Friends,

Family And

Other F*ck

Ups

Because Therapy Is Expensive and Wine
Only Goes So Far

CONTENTS

Family: The Baggage Claim You Never Asked For
Some families hand you heirlooms.
Others hand you emotional baggage and expect you to carry
it forever.
The truth? We don't choose the suitcase we're given at birth.
We just get stuck dragging it through airports, reunions,
and group chats—
wondering why it's always overweight and leaking some-
thing weird.
Welcome to the guide for surviving the people you can't
escape.
Handle with humor. Handle with wine. Handle with care.

For the friends and relatives who will inevitably ask, "Is this about me?" The answer is yes.

FOREWORD

*by Dr. Penelope Hargreaves, Author of **Why Your Family Is Ruining Your Life***

When I was asked to write the foreword for *Friends, Family, and Other Fck Ups,** my first thought was, *"I Love It" A book brave enough to say what we're all screaming into our pillows."* My second thought was, *"Who keeps inviting Aunt Carol to potlucks when all she brings is trauma?"*

As a bestselling author of several highly unnecessary self-help books—including *Stop Apologizing to Your Plants* and *How to Gaslight Your Dog Into Thinking You're the Alpha*—I consider myself uniquely unqualified to comment on healthy relationships. And yet, I can say with absolute certainty that this book is the closest thing we'll ever get to a survival manual for the dysfunctional humans we didn't choose but are stuck with anyway.

The brilliance here is twofold:

It's honest. No sugar-coating, no fake smiles, no pretending Thanksgiving dinner isn't a hostage negotiation with cranberry sauce.

It's funny. And let's face it, if you can't laugh at the fact your cousin believes pigeons are government drones, you'll end up crying into your boxed wine.

This book doesn't promise to heal your relationships, fix your family, or stop the Drama Queen from sighing like she's auditioning for a soap opera. What it *does* promise is survival—and, if you're lucky, a laugh big enough to drown out the sound of your Drunk Uncle trying karaoke.

So read this book. Dog-ear the pages. Keep it handy at every gathering. Because while therapy is expensive and wine only goes so far, this manual is cheaper, funnier, and far more satisfying than throwing mashed potatoes at your in-laws (though I'm not saying don't try that).

Welcome, dear reader, to the only Olympic sport you didn't sign up for but must compete in anyway: surviving the people you can't escape.

Sincerely,

Dr. Penelope Hargreaves
Author, Speaker, and Survivor of Four Consecutive Thanksgiving "Incidents"

Introduction: Why This Book Exists (And Why You Need It)

The Myth of the Perfect Circle

Every circle has its quirks. Some are tiny, like a friend who insists on explaining crypto at brunch, or a coworker who reheats fish in the office microwave. Others are massive, like a cousin who's been "finding themselves" for 27 years or a roommate who still thinks dish soap is optional. Put them all together and what you get isn't a wholesome holiday photo—it's a never-ending blooper reel nobody asked to be in.

And yet, everyone pretends. Pretends their family is functional, their friendships are drama-free, their coworkers are tolerable. Pretends Christmas dinner is joyful instead of a hostage negotiation with cranberry sauce. Pretends Friendsgiving is about gratitude instead of barely suppressed rage over who "forgot" to Venmo for the turkey. Pretends weddings are about love instead of open-air auditions for "Most Inappropriate Toast."

The truth? Perfect people don't exist—and perfect groups definitely don't. That "bestie squad" with the matching selfies? Someone's blocking someone before dessert. That family with the matching pajamas on Instagram? They're hiding a screaming match that happened two seconds before the picture. That office team who "gets along beautifully"? Someone's hoarding a grudge about a stolen stapler from 1994.

Across cultures, the dysfunction just wears different costumes. Italian relatives yell across the table with love (and also actual yelling). British friends bury everything under politeness until the eventual explosion makes the tabloids. American coworkers pretend team-building retreats will fix it all, while scheduling Zoom calls guaranteed to undo any progress. Meanwhile, your grandma is muttering that "none of this would happen if people still respected Jell-O molds."

And generationally? It's chaos. Boomers critique your life choices while Gen Z live-streams the fight on TikTok. Millennials try to keep the peace with charcuterie boards, while Gen X mutters in the corner, "I knew this would happen." Dysfunction adapts, evolves, and marches forward like a family heirloom nobody wanted but everyone inherited.

That's why this book exists. Because once you stop pretending your family, friends, and assorted humans are perfect—or could ever be perfect—you're free. Free to laugh at the absurdity. Free to roast the people who deserve it. Free to stop expecting "normal" and start embracing "oh my God, did that just happen?" as the baseline.

Sneak Previews of Dysfunction

If this book were a reality show, here's the cast list. You've already met them in your own life—you just didn't have the words for their brand of chaos until now.

The Drama Queen

Not just family. This could be your roommate, coworker, or that one friend who turns every papercut into a Broadway finale.

The Moocher

Treats your fridge, wallet, or Wi-Fi like it's a public utility. Somehow never has their own charger but always leaves with your leftovers.

The Drunk Uncle (Or Friend, Or Colleague)

Equal parts comedian, philosopher, and HR violation. Three drinks away from falling asleep in the dip or oversharing a story that nobody needed.

The Guilt Tripper

Doesn't need alcohol—they've weaponized sighing. Family, friend, or colleague, they drop guilt grenades that leave you apologizing for things you didn't do.

The Toxic Friend

Not technically family but might as well be. Texts feel like emotional subpoenas. Their loyalty is really just chaos in a trench coat.

The In-Law Olympics

Dating, marrying, or even *befriending* someone new means competing in events you never trained for: casserole competitions, parenting critiques, unsolicited advice. The scoring system is rigged.

The Social Media Show-Off

Everything's a photoshoot. Every dish is cold because they needed the perfect overhead shot. Every tag is a fresh humiliation where you look like a goblin while they look like an influencer.

And that's just a taste. We haven't even gotten to the Conspiracy Cousins, the Creepy Coworkers, or the friends who think your boundaries are just "suggestions." Think of this book as a safari guide—you'll recognize the creatures, laugh at their Classic Moves, and learn how to survive their natural habitats.

The Survival Philosophy

Here's the deal: these people aren't going to change. They've rehearsed these roles like veteran actors in a long-running soap opera. Your uncle won't discover boundaries. Your roommate won't suddenly clean up. Your best friend won't quit oversharing their toxic relationship. Dysfunction isn't something you fix—it's something you outwit.

And the best weapon? Humor.

Because you can't argue someone out of being a Drama Queen. You can't guilt the Guilt Tripper into stopping (they'll just out-guilt you). But you *can* laugh. Laughter turns dysfunction into comedy instead of tragedy.

This book doesn't promise miracle cures. What you'll find are coping strategies—some practical, some sarcastic. You'll learn to spot the Classic Moves, fake a phone call during the Silent Treatment, weaponize sarcasm against the Social Media Show-Off, and maybe even turn their antics into entertainment.

Think of this as your dysfunctional-life field manual. Soldiers go into battle with maps and strategies; you're going into weddings, reunions, and group chats with this book. When your friend texts a 2 a.m. guilt bomb, you'll know you've just been hit with the Toxic Friend's move. When your uncle faceplants into the mashed potatoes, you won't cry—you'll add it to the highlight reel.

The philosophy is simple: stop expecting normal. Once you drop the illusion, you stop being disappointed. Dysfunction isn't the end of the world—it's the start of a really good story.

And let's be real—the disasters are what people bond over. Nobody retells "everything went smoothly." The stories that stick are the turkey fires, the drunken toasts, the awkward roommate feuds, the group chats gone nuclear. Those are the moments that make up life with people.

So no, this book won't fix your family, friends, or colleagues. But it *will* give you permission to laugh at them, roast them, and survive them with your sanity (mostly) intact.

Before we dive in, let's be clear: dysfunction doesn't stop at bloodlines. Oh no. It leaks. It spreads. It multiplies. Sure, you've got your family weirdos—the Drama Queens, the Drunk Uncles, the Guilt Trippers—but then come the outsiders. The Toxic Friend who calls at midnight with their latest crisis. The Social

Media Show-Off who drags you into their content machine. The in-laws who treat every gathering like an Olympic sport. Even coworkers sometimes sneak into the mix, lurking at weddings and potlucks with opinions nobody asked for.

Basically, if you're in a group of humans, dysfunction is guaranteed. Friends, in-laws, neighbors, that "family friend" who just shows up to every barbecue even though no one remembers inviting them—they're all part of the extended cast. This isn't just a family guide. It's a *people guide*. Because let's face it: if you're reading this, you don't need help dealing with one person—you need help surviving the entire ecosystem.

So here's your disclaimer: this book will not fix anyone. It won't stop the Moocher from raiding your fridge, it won't keep your aunt from sighing dramatically, and it definitely won't prevent your cousin from posting live updates of your holiday meltdown on Instagram. But it *will* make you laugh. It will give you language, so you can name the chaos instead of just drowning in it. It will give you permission to roll your eyes, walk away, and maybe even enjoy the show.

This isn't therapy. This isn't healing. This is survival through humor. It's a roast disguised as a guidebook. It's solidarity in sarcasm. It's proof that you're not the only one thinking, *Wow, my family/friends/in-laws are completely insane.* Because everyone's are.

So consider this your survival manual. Your handbook. Your field guide. Your permission slip to laugh instead of cry, roast instead of rage, survive instead of spiral.

Now grab a drink, loosen your waistband, and let's get into it. Welcome to the dysfunctional circus. The lights are on, the stage is set, and the weirdos are waiting.

CHAPTER ONE
THE DRAMA QUEEN

Every family has one. Every friend group has one. The Drama Queen.

They don't just live life—they *star* in it. And not in a cool, Oscar-winning way. This is low-budget soap opera territory, the kind with wobbly sets and terrible acting, where someone faints in every episode and the cliffhanger revolves around whether Karen's latte had too much foam.

You know exactly who I'm talking about. The one who texts *"Call me, it's an emergency"* and when you panic and ring back, the "emergency" is that their Wi-Fi cut out in the middle of *Love*

Island. The one who sighs so loudly at dinner you think they've been mortally wounded, only to announce that the chicken is "a little dry." The one who makes a dentist appointment sound like a season finale.

Drama Queens are allergic to peace. Give them a calm afternoon and they'll inject it with chaos like it's Botox. Free holiday to Hawaii? Too humid. First-class seat? The champagne was "luke-warm." Brand new phone? Wrong shade of pink—it clashes with their aura. Stubbed toe? Not just a stub—it's basically a compound fracture requiring immediate prayer circles.

And here's the cruel joke: Drama Queens don't actually want solutions. They don't want perspective. They don't want calm. What they want is an audience. *Your* audience. You didn't audition for season 47 of *Their Life: The Tragedy Continues,* but congratulations—you've been cast as the unwilling sidekick, applause not optional.

They are emotional arsonists. If there's no drama, they'll manufacture it. If there's no disaster, they'll invent one. They light small matches in ordinary moments just to watch them go up in flames. The rest of us are left choking on the smoke, clutching our drinks, and wondering how spilled gravy turned into an international crisis.

And if you're sitting there smugly thinking, *"Ha, my family doesn't have one of those,"* I've got bad news for you. Look in the mirror, friend. If you can't spot the Drama Queen at the table, chances are, it's you.

The Classic Moves

Drama Queens don't experience life the way normal humans do. Where you see a slight inconvenience, they see a global crisis worthy of a press conference.

A barista forgets their extra pump of vanilla. That's grounds for emotional collapse. A minor headache? They're writing their will. You'd think they'd been struck by lightning, when in reality, they just had to stand in line at Target for more than five minutes.

They operate on a different scale of measurement. Rain on their wedding day isn't bad luck—it's a conspiracy. A flight delay isn't a nuisance—it's a hostage situation. A "low battery" warning on their phone isn't an alert—it's the beginning of the apocalypse.

And God help you if you don't play along. Fail to gasp appropriately at their tale of injustice and you've just been cast as the villain in their story. You'll be the "unsupportive sibling," the "heartless friend," or worse, the "monster who didn't even care when my soy milk was lukewarm."

Drama Queens also have a special gift for timing. They don't melt down when you're free on a Saturday afternoon. No, their preferred stage is when you're late for work, about to board a flight, or mid-bite at Thanksgiving dinner. Because what's better than ruining your day while making sure they're the center of attention?

And don't think for a second that their performance ends when the drama does. Oh no. Drama Queens are master archivists. Every tiny slight, every perceived wound, every overblown crisis is carefully filed away so they can bring it up again and again. They don't let things go—they build sequels.

For them, life isn't one long story. It's a series of reruns, each one featuring their greatest hits. "Remember that time the waiter gave me tap water instead of sparkling? I'll never recover." Spoiler: they did recover. In fact, they left a one-star Yelp review to make sure everyone else knew about their suffering too.

How to Survive the Drama Queen

Now, let's be clear. You can't cure a Drama Queen. You can't fix them. You can't reason with them. You can only survive them. Think of it less like a relationship and more like wilderness survival training. You don't tame a tornado—you just board up your windows, grab snacks, and hope your insurance covers emotional damage.

Here are your essential tools:

The Nod-and-Smile Technique

Perfected by generations of weary relatives who have suffered before you, this technique is the backbone of Drama Queen survival. Just nod, smile, and let your brain float off to a safe place, like imagining you're on a beach without Wi-Fi, or visualizing what it would be like to live inside a quiet library. The Drama Queen thinks you're engaged, but in reality you're mentally reorganizing your sock drawer.

The Emotional Earplugs

Not actual earplugs—although, frankly, that wouldn't hurt. Emotional earplugs are about detachment. You don't need to hear every microscopic detail about how Susan's coworker "stole her stapler energy." You don't need to absorb the fury of a latte made with 2% instead of almond milk. Picture their words bouncing harmlessly off your mental windshield. Nod occasionally, maybe toss in a "Wow, that sounds tough," and let the nonsense pass you by.

Emergency Snacks

When the Drama Queen ramps up, you ramp up your chewing. Keep chocolate, chips, pretzels, or anything edible within arm's reach. Not for them—for you. Snacks provide a physical coping mechanism: something to bite down on while you resist the urge to scream. Studies* show that chewing reduces stress by 63%. (*Studies = me, hiding in the pantry with a family-size bag of Doritos.)

Strategic Exits

Drama Queens are hunters, and their prey is your attention. Always know where the exits are. Map the room the moment you enter: back door, bathroom, even a conveniently timed "Oh no, I left something in the car." Bonus tactic: bring your phone charger and periodically announce, "I need to plug this in." Boom—five minutes of sweet freedom.

The Forbidden Phrase

Never—and I mean never—say *"calm down."* You might as well light a match in a fireworks factory. That phrase guarantees you've just purchased a front-row ticket to a three-act meltdown with no intermission. The only thing worse is saying, *"You're overreacting."* If those words leave your mouth, start looking for emergency exits immediately.

The Scapegoat Shuffle

Identify another relative in the room and subtly redirect the Drama Queen toward them. "Wow, that's wild. You should really tell Aunt Carol—she *loves* stories like this." Release them into the wild and slip away before they notice.

The Distraction Device

When things get truly unbearable, pull out your phone. Not to scroll—too obvious. Use it as a prop. "Oh no, I've got to reply to this, it's urgent." Nobody needs to know you're fake emailing yourself recipes or Googling "how to survive a dinner with a Drama Queen."

The Zen of Acceptance

Eventually, you reach a stage of inner peace. You stop expecting the Drama Queen to change. You stop waiting for a calm meal. You stop praying for logic. Instead, you embrace it. They'll wail, they'll sigh, they'll collapse onto the couch like an understudy auditioning for a telenovela. And you? You'll sip your wine, crunch your chips, and think: *Well, at least it's never boring.*

Final Rule of Survival: It's not your job to fix the Drama Queen. It's not even your job to keep them happy. Your job is to minimize collateral damage, escape when necessary, and live to tell the tale. Accept that they will always be starring in a show you didn't audition for. Your role is simple: don't let them drag you into the plot.

The Wrap-Up

At the end of the day, Drama Queens are exhausting, ridiculous, and utterly predictable. You can set your watch by their meltdowns. They'll be there at every holiday, every dinner, every vacation—ready to transform spilled gravy into a Shakespearean tragedy, or a mild inconvenience into a three-act opera complete with tears, sighs, and a dramatic exit toward the bathroom.

Yes, you'll roll your eyes. You'll sigh deeply. You'll practice the ancient art of the fake smile while whispering *"please let this be over soon"* into your mashed potatoes. But once the chaos passes and the dust settles, you'll realize something inconvenient: as much as you can't stand them, you also can't quite imagine the circus without them.

Because let's be honest—without the Drama Queen, your family gatherings would be... boring. Nobody remembers the smooth dinner or the polite conversation. People bond over disasters, over the turkey fire, over the time Aunt Carol accused the cranberry sauce of "ruining her life." Drama Queens provide the disasters that fuel the stories you'll retell for decades.

And they love the stage. If drama were frequent flyer miles, they'd already be in first class, sipping champagne and sighing loudly that the bubbles are "too aggressive." Meanwhile, the rest of us are stuck at the gate, wondering how we got dragged into this trip, clutching our carry-ons full of unresolved resentment.

Here's the irony: for all their noise, Drama Queens are reliable. They'll always deliver. You never have to worry that a gathering will be too quiet, too uneventful, or too peaceful. The Drama Queen has your back. They'll cry if nobody else does, they'll faint if attention wavers, and they'll fight with the waiter just to keep the adrenaline pumping.

So the next time the Drama Queen launches into a monologue about being "deeply wounded" by a poorly carved ham, don't panic. Just sit back, grab a drink, and remind yourself: this is free entertainment. You didn't buy tickets, but you're front row at a show that never gets canceled. And in its own twisted way, that's kind of a gift.

CHAPTER TWO
THE OVERSHARER

The Oversharer is easy to spot. In fact, you can't miss them. They're the ones unloading their entire medical history while you're just trying to buy milk. You don't so much talk to them as endure a TED Talk you never asked for—complete with bonus slides about their rash.

There is no warm-up, no context, no easing you in. One second, you're standing in line, minding your own business. The next, they've cornered you with a confession about their failed marriage, their cholesterol numbers, and what their cat coughed up that morning. And all you said was, "Hi."

Oversharers are like human podcasts on shuffle. You never know what episode you're going to get. One day it's "My Root Canal: The Untold Story." The next day it's "Why My Boss Hates Me and Probably Always Has." And if you're really lucky, you'll get "My Most Intimate Secrets, Volume 12." No subscription required.

They live by one rule: *If it's in my head, it's coming out of my mouth.* And that would be fine—if they knew when to stop. But they don't. They never do. The Oversharer isn't just giving you highlights; they're giving you the uncut director's commentary.

The worst part? They *think* they're being relatable. They believe they're building connection by telling you how their cousin's ex-boyfriend's dog has anxiety. They're not. They're building a wall of noise so high you could climb it, rappel down the other side, and they'd still be talking about their colon.

You don't need to know about their medication dosage. You don't need to know about the mole that "looks kinda funky." You don't need to know about the dream they had where their teeth fell out and Harry Styles handed them a pickle. But guess what? You're going to know. You're going to know it all.

Oversharers are like Netflix autoplay—you didn't choose it, you didn't want it, but suddenly you're eight episodes in, and now you know way too much about Sheila's hysterectomy.

And don't think you can escape. Oversharers are relentless. They will follow you from the kitchen to the bathroom door, narrating the details of their breakup while you frantically search for an excuse. "Oh, you're busy? Don't worry, I'll be quick," they say, right before launching into the 27-part saga of their gym membership cancellation.

Every family has one. Every office has one. Every friend group has one. And if you can't think of who yours is—well, then it might be time to check yourself. (Hint: if you've already texted your friends three paragraphs today about your morning smoothie, the call is coming from inside the house.)

Oversharers are not dangerous, exactly. But they are exhausting. Spending time with one is like being waterboarded with unnecessary details. It's not that you're going to drown—it's that you're going to wish you had.

The Classic Moves

The Oversharer doesn't just tell stories; they weaponize them. They take the kind of information most of us bury deep in the vault of "things only my doctor needs to know" and serve it up like hors d'oeuvres at a cocktail party.

They'll drop sentences like, "Well, ever since my hemorrhoid surgery..." in the middle of your lunch. You choke on your sandwich, but they keep going, describing the stitches with a level of detail that would make a surgeon blush.

They'll lean across the table at a wedding reception to tell you about their yeast infection. Right as you're lifting a forkful of cake. That's an Oversharer's superpower: timing. They can sniff out the exact moment you're most vulnerable and strike like a confessional assassin.

And the problem is, they don't just stop at the headline. No, no. Oversharers give you the *full documentary*. If it's about their bad date, you're not just getting "it didn't go well." You're getting what he ordered, what shirt he wore, what his ex texted him mid-dinner, what time they left, how she felt about his shoes, and—bonus—screenshots of the texts he sent afterward. You didn't ask, but guess what? It's in your brain now.

Social media has only made them worse. Oversharers treat Facebook like it's a 24-hour broadcast channel and you're their only subscriber. They're the ones posting 47 updates a day, complete with photos of their meals, their workouts, and their child's potty-training progress. Yes, Brenda, we're all thrilled that little Timmy finally pooped. Please stop posting photographic evidence.

And don't even get me started on family group chats. Oversharers treat those like personal therapy journals. While you're trying to coordinate Thanksgiving dinner, they're dumping six paragraphs about how their boss "doesn't appreciate their energy." You scroll, scroll, scroll, looking for the part about who's bringing the stuffing, but all you find is a detailed rant about Steve from accounting.

Oversharers also have no shame in public. You'll be at a café, trying to enjoy your coffee, when you overhear someone describing their colonoscopy in surround sound. And it's not just the friend across from them who's hearing it—you, the barista, the couple on a date, and probably the entire Yelp review audience are now in on it too.

And if you think pretending not to listen will save you, think again. Oversharers crave validation. If you're not nodding, they'll rope you in with, "Right? Don't you think?" Suddenly, you're forced to give an opinion about whether their ex's new girlfriend really is "a troll."

The truth is, Oversharers are emotional streakers. They're running through life butt-naked, shouting their business to anyone within earshot. You don't want to see it, you don't want to know it, but now it's burned into your memory forever.

How to Survive the Oversharer

Surviving the Oversharer isn't about shutting them down—because that's impossible. These people could find a way to narrate their own autopsy if you let them. No, survival is about managing exposure, like sunburn or secondhand smoke. Here's how.

1. Perfect the Strategic Nod

You don't have to listen. You don't even have to care. You just have to nod at the right intervals so they think you're tuned in. Tilt your head slightly, make the occasional "Mmm" sound, and they'll keep talking. It's like winding up a toy—you just need to jiggle the key every now and then, and off they go. Meanwhile, you can mentally plan your grocery list or fantasize about moving to a cave with no Wi-Fi.

2. Fake an Emergency

Oversharers don't care if you're busy—they assume you're desperate to hear about the new cream they're using for their toenail fungus. So you need an escape plan. Keep your phone on vibrate and be ready to gasp, "Oh no, I've got to take this, it's urgent." You don't need an actual call. Oversharers never check. They're too busy reliving the time their cousin's neighbor's hamster got lost in the dryer.

3. Play the Reverse Overshare

Fight fire with fire. When they tell you about their embarrassing medical condition, hit them back with one of your own—real or made up. "Oh wow, your root canal sounds awful. Did I ever tell you about the time I accidentally glued my eyelid shut with superglue?" Oversharers aren't used to competition. Sometimes the only way to shut them up is to horrify them more than they horrify you.

4. The Bathroom Break Defense

Never underestimate the power of pretending you desperately need the bathroom. No one questions it, and it gives you at least five minutes of sweet, blessed silence. If they try to follow you? Lock the door. Oversharers have no shame, but even they usually won't narrate through a bathroom stall. Usually.

5. Redirect with Questions They Can't Answer

Oversharers love easy topics: breakups, rashes, exes, bosses. Flip the script. Ask them something technical like, "Can you explain quantum mechanics?" or "How would you fix America's tax system?" Watch their brain short-circuit while you back away slowly.

6. Create a Decoy Audience

If you're trapped in a group setting, the trick is to redirect their fire onto someone else. Oversharers are like heat-seeking missiles for attention. All you have to do is casually say, "Oh, hey, didn't Sarah go through something similar?" Boom. Target acquired. You're free. Sarah, however, is not. Sorry, Sarah.

7. Accept That Escape Is Sometimes Futile

Here's the grim truth: sometimes there is no way out. You just have to ride the storm. Let them talk. Let them unload. Let them explain, in excruciating detail, how they once had a hangnail that "changed their life." Then, once they've exhausted themselves, quietly slip away like a ninja.

Oversharer Bingo

Because sometimes you learn more about your relatives in five minutes than you ever wanted to know in a lifetime. Keep this card handy when Aunt Linda starts talking about her bunions.

Bingo Squares:

Mentions a medical condition in graphic detail.

Starts a sentence with *"Not to overshare, but..."* and then overshares.

Talks about their bathroom habits (in public, mid-meal).

Shares intimate marital/relationship drama with the whole table.

Brings up therapy breakthroughs to people who didn't ask.

Whispers something scandalous... loudly enough for the whole room to hear.

Reveals how much money they make (or don't).

Overshares about childbirth in horrifying detail.

Discusses pets' digestive issues during dinner.

Tells a deeply personal story about a coworker no one knows.

Confesses a wild secret and then says, *"Don't tell anyone."*

TMI about their last surgery/procedure.

Volunteers unsolicited details about their sex life (bonus if visual).

Drunkenly admits something they *really* shouldn't.

Ends with, *"Wow, I don't know why I told you all that."*

Bonus Square:

Shout *"Bingo!"* if they use the phrase *"We're basically family, so I can tell you this..."* right before traumatizing everyone.

The Wrap-Up

The Oversharer isn't evil. They're not hatching a master plan to ruin your day. They're not criminal masterminds—they're just social pickpockets, robbing you of your peace one unnecessary detail at a time. They can't help it. It's a compulsion. Where most of us feel a little voice whisper, "Hmm, maybe keep that to yourself," the Oversharer hears, "Quick, say it louder!"

And that's the tragedy: they think they're bonding. They believe that by telling you about their cousin's third divorce, their botched tattoo, and the time they accidentally peed in an elevator, they're making you feel closer. What they're actually doing is making you wish you had noise-canceling headphones surgically installed.

Oversharers are the living embodiment of TMI. They blur the line between casual chat and hostage situation. You'll start a conversation thinking you're safe, and twenty minutes later you'll know more about their digestion than their own doctor does. And the worst part? You'll never forget it. These stories burn into your brain like permanent tattoos. Years from now, you'll be lying in bed, minding your own business, when the mental image of their uncle's bunion surgery kicks down the door.

Here's the harsh truth: there's no escape. Not really. You can dodge their calls, mute their texts, and feign emergencies, but sooner or later you'll be cornered again. That's the Oversharer guarantee. They are like glitter—you think you've shaken them off, but somehow, they stick around forever, showing up in places you least expect.

So, what do you do? You accept your fate. You laugh about it later. You tell your own friends about the ridiculous things you've been forced to hear, turning their oversharing into your entertainment. Because if you can't laugh at it, you'll cry—and then they'll probably tell you about the time *they* cried harder, louder, and longer.

In the end, the Oversharer is part of the ecosystem. Annoying? Absolutely. Draining? Always. But secretly kind of useful? Yes. Because without them, you wouldn't have half the stories you tell at your own parties. They're like human content generators—infuriating in the moment, but gold for your comedy material.

So nod, smile, escape when you can, and remember: oversharing is their Olympic sport. You're just a spectator, whether you bought tickets or not.

Chapter Three
The Moocher

Ah, the Moocher. You know exactly who I mean. The friend who "forgets their wallet." The cousin who "just needs to borrow twenty bucks until Friday" and then mysteriously vanishes every Friday for the rest of eternity. The coworker who's somehow always out of coffee pods but always in your kitchen making themselves at home.

The Moocher is the human version of a black hole. No matter how much you give, they will suck it all in, smile, and somehow convince you to hand over more. They're not just broke—they're *professionally broke*. It's an identity, a lifestyle, a full-time hustle.

Let's be clear: everyone has hard times. Everyone needs a little help now and then. But the Moocher? They've turned it into an Olympic sport. They can sniff out generosity the way sharks smell blood in the water. You make the mistake of offering once—one little, tiny loan, one "Sure, I'll cover dinner this time"—and congratulations, you've just been recruited into their personal welfare program.

The Moocher is an expert in excuses. Their wallet is always in their "other jacket." Their card is always "acting weird." Their bank is always "processing something." They have more reasons than a politician dodging questions. And somehow, no matter what happens, they're always broke—but not too broke for new sneakers, weekend trips, or the latest iPhone.

Meals with a Moocher follow a predictable pattern. You order, they order twice as much, and when the check arrives, they suddenly develop an urgent need to use the bathroom. Ten minutes later, you're staring at the bill, realizing you just bought Derek three margaritas and a lobster tail while you ate nachos.

It's not just money, either. The Moocher lives to borrow. They'll "just borrow" your sweater, your charger, your Netflix password, your car. They'll take anything not nailed down, and sometimes even things that are. They never return what they borrow, but they'll happily remind you what else they still need. If you've ever found yourself yelling, "Hey, is that my hoodie?" across a crowded bar, you've been Moochered.

The worst part is, they don't even feel guilty. In fact, they act like you should feel honored. Like covering their rent or letting them crash on your couch is some kind of sacred privilege. Moochers are allergic to shame. They'll show up to your house, eat your food, drink your wine, and still complain that you don't have the "good" snacks.

And God forbid you ever say no. If you do, they'll look at you like you just punted a puppy across the street. They'll sigh, tell you how "hard things are right now," and make you feel like the villain in their personal sob story. Next thing you know, you're apologizing—for not giving them your last $20.

Moochers are like vampires, but instead of blood, they suck up your cash, your energy, your patience, and your Netflix recommendations. And like vampires, once they're invited in, they're impossible to get rid of.

Here's the thing: every family has one. Sometimes, an unlucky friend group has *three*. If you're lucky, you only see yours on holidays. If you're unlucky, they're your roommate. And if you're really unlucky, they're your kid.

And if you're reading this thinking, "Huh, nobody in my circle acts like that," then brace yourself baby. Either you're the luckiest human alive... or maybe, just maybe, you're the Moocher.

The Classic Moves

Moochers have a sixth sense for free stuff. You could whisper "open bar" in another state, and they'd materialize at the venue like a magician's trick. Mention "leftovers" and they'll already be in your kitchen with Tupperware, scooping lasagna before you've even had seconds.

Invite them to a potluck? Don't bother. Their contribution will be a half-empty bag of chips they "found in the car," or worse, they'll show up with nothing but a smile and a story about how they were *just too busy* to cook. But don't worry—they'll make up for it by demolishing half the spread and taking a plate home "for later."

Moochers also love vacations. Not paying for them, of course—just tagging along on yours. They'll crash in your hotel room, eat your complimentary breakfast, and then complain about how the pillows aren't fluffy enough. And the kicker? They'll tell people *they* took a trip, like they booked the whole thing themselves. You footed the bill, but they get the Instagram clout.

And oh, the excuses. Moochers can deliver them with Oscar-worthy conviction. Their wallet? Always in their other pants. Their card? Always declined "by mistake." Their bank? Always running "fraud checks." Meanwhile, somehow, they've got money for VIP concert tickets, a new gaming console, or an endless supply of vape pods. Funny how that works.

Borrowing is their native language. They don't ask to borrow—they announce it. "I'll just grab this hoodie, okay?" is not a question, it's a declaration. And you'll never see that hoodie again. If you do, it'll be on them, stretched two sizes bigger, with a mysterious stain that looks suspiciously like nacho cheese.

Tech gear? Forget it. Chargers, headphones, spare remotes—once a Moocher gets their hands on it, consider it a donation. You'll ask for it back, and they'll hit you with, "Oh yeah, I think I left it at my cousin's place." Translation: gone forever.

And don't even get me started on the check dance at restaurants. Moochers will happily order the most expensive thing on the menu, throw in a round of drinks, and then pull the classic,

"Oh no, I didn't realize it was going to be split evenly." Yes, Derek, you did. You always do.

Family Moochers are the sneakiest. They disguise themselves as "poor little me." They'll drop lines like, "You know I'm struggling right now" while standing in their brand-new sneakers. Or they'll remind you how "family takes care of family," right before borrowing your car and returning it with the fuel light blinking.

The truth is, Moochers are opportunists. They'll take whatever you're dumb enough to give and act like it's your civic duty to keep giving. To them, generosity is weakness, and your wallet is basically a public resource.

How to Survive the Moocher

You can't reform a Moocher. You can't inspire them to "do better." This is not a growth journey—it's a containment strategy. Your job isn't to save them. Your job is to protect yourself, your wallet, and your fridge.

1. Go Cash-Only Around Them

Moochers thrive on plastic. The "Oh, I'll pay you back later" promise is their bread and butter. Solution? Don't give them the option. When you go out, bring cash—just enough for yourself. No extras. No wiggle room. When the bill comes and they start with, "Hey, can you spot me?" you can wave your empty wallet and say, "Sorry, man, I'm tapped out." Watching the panic spread across their face is almost worth the hassle.

2. Label Everything in Your House

Moochers are like raccoons—they'll rummage through your stuff and walk off with whatever's shiny. Stop them with labels.

Slap your name on chargers, snacks, hoodies—everything. The more childish the label looks, the better. Bonus points if you use glitter pens. Nothing kills a Moocher's buzz like explaining to their date why their phone charger says "PROPERTY OF KAREN – HANDS OFF."

3. Master the Art of the Silent Stare

Sometimes words aren't enough. When they start with, "I'll get you back next time," don't argue. Just... stare. Long. Silent. Unblinking. Moochers are uncomfortable with accountability. A few seconds of icy eye contact can be more effective than a thousand lectures.

4. The Booby-Trap Fridge Method

This one takes commitment. Moochers love to raid fridges, so make yours a danger zone. Leave unlabeled containers of mystery leftovers. Fill a Tupperware with kale and expired hummus. Put a sticky note on the pizza box that says, "Contains laxatives." It doesn't matter if it's true—it only matters that it buys you time.

5. Pretend You're Broke Too

The Moocher's kryptonite is another Moocher. Hit them with their own lines: "Oh no, my card's not working right now," or, "My bank's holding my money for review." Watch them glitch like a computer on low battery. Two Moochers in the same room is like two dogs staring at one bone. Nobody wins.

6. Introduce Them to Another Moocher

Advanced move, not for beginners. Pair your Moocher with another Moocher and let them bleed each other dry. It's like setting up a blind date that ends in mutual bankruptcy.

7. Say the Forbidden Word

It's terrifying. It's powerful. And it works. The word is: "No." Moochers hate it. They'll pout, whine, maybe even try guilt-tripping you, but remember this—every "no" is one step closer to freedom. Practice it in the mirror if you have to. Channel your inner bouncer. Protect your boundaries like they're the last fries in the bag.

At the end of the day, Moochers only exist because people let them. Stop feeding them, stop funding them, and suddenly they're powerless. They'll move on to the next poor soul, leaving you with a lighter conscience and, finally, a fridge full of snacks that belong to you.

Moocher Bingo

Next time The Moocher shows up, pull out this card and play along. First one to get five in a row wins the satisfaction of being right all along.

Squares:

Arrives "forgetting" their wallet.

Asks, *"You gonna finish that?"*

Leaves with leftovers in your Tupperware (which never comes back).

Orders the most expensive thing, then offers to "split evenly."

Borrows a hoodie, mysteriously never returns it.

Drinks all your beer but claims they "don't drink much."

Volunteers to "help with gas," hands you a single coin.

Casually asks for your Netflix password "just until payday."

Claims Venmo/Cash App "isn't working right now."

Shows up uninvited when food is involved.

Insists they'll "get the next round." Spoiler: they won't.

"Forgets" to bring anything to potlucks. Always leaves with dessert.

Bonus: Yell *"Bingo!"* when they eye your fries. They'll deny it, then eat them anyway.

The Wrap-Up

The Moocher is living proof that some people are born with talent—and theirs just happens to be freeloading. Forget musical ability, athletic skill, or academic brilliance. Their gift is showing up empty-handed and leaving with leftovers. They can sniff out free food three suburbs away. They can materialize at a barbecue you didn't even invite them to, plate in hand, already eyeing the Tupperware. They have the uncanny ability to charm their way into your wallet, borrow your charger "just for a sec," and somehow make *you* believe it was your idea to cover their half of the bill.

They're less a person and more a lifestyle parasite. If oxygen cost money, the Moocher would already be standing next to you saying, *"Hey, could you spot me a couple breaths?"*

And here's the brutal truth: Moochers never disappear. You can dodge their calls, block their number, change your locks, and they'll still find a way back in. They're like human glitter—you think you've shaken them off, but six months later they've reappeared in your living room, holding a tote bag and asking if you've got "any spare snacks."

They show up at your door with tragic stories, sad faces, and just enough guilt to make you hand over your last slice of pizza. That's their true genius: they make you feel like *you're* the selfish one for not funding their nonsense. They turn basic self-preservation into cruelty. Suddenly, refusing to hand over your hoodie is the emotional equivalent of pushing a puppy into traffic.

So let's be clear: Moochers don't need your charity. They need boundaries. They need a reality check. And they definitely need to start buying their own damn margaritas. Until then, keep your wallet close, your hoodie hidden, and your fridge booby-trapped.

Because if you let them, they'll take everything—your fries, your dignity, and probably your Netflix password. And nobody forgives fry theft. Nobody.

Chapter Four
The One-Upper

If you've ever shared good news, only to have someone immediately hijack it with a story about how *their* experience was bigger, better, or twice as impressive—congratulations, you've met the One-Upper.

You tell them you ran a 5K. They ran a marathon. You bought a new car. They bought a better car, for less money, with better mileage. You mention you're tired. They've been awake since 1994. Whatever you've done, they've done it harder, faster, longer, and with more Instagram likes.

The One-Upper's entire personality is based on outshining everyone else. They can't let anyone else have the spotlight, even for a second. If you're sick, they're sicker. If you're happy, they're happier. If you're sad, they've been through *way worse.* It's not a conversation with them—it's a competition. And guess what? You're always losing.

These people don't celebrate your victories. They repackage them into their own victories. You say, "I finally got a promotion at work!" Instead of saying "Congrats!" they hit you with, "Oh, I remember when I got *my* big promotion, except mine came with a huge raise, a better office, and a company car." Suddenly, your exciting news is reduced to crumbs while they've baked themselves a three-tier victory cake.

The One-Upper doesn't just want to be good. They want to be better than you. They treat every anecdote like a race, every story like a duel, and every achievement like a scoreboard where they must always be on top. It's exhausting.

Family One-Uppers are the worst. You tell your aunt you're cooking Thanksgiving dinner for ten people, and she immediately brags about how she once cooked for fifty, during a blackout, with only one working burner. You could climb Mount Everest tomorrow and your cousin would still find a way to one-up you by reminding everyone that they once climbed "a much harder mountain" while fasting.

It's not just achievements, either. They'll one-up misery, too. You mention your back hurts, and suddenly they've got full-blown sciatica. You say you're stressed, and they're having a nervous breakdown. You say you barely slept, and they've been surviving on thirty minutes of sleep a week since high school. It's like having a competition you never signed up for—and losing is guaranteed.

The worst part is, they don't even realize how unbearable they are. To them, they're just "sharing their story." In reality, they're sucking the joy out of everyone else's. Every conversation with them is like being stuck in a never-ending Olympics of nonsense, where no matter what you've done, they've already set a world record.

If you've ever walked away from a chat feeling like your win didn't matter, your pain wasn't valid, or your story wasn't impressive enough, congratulations—you've been one-upped. And you'll be one-upped again, and again, until you learn the art of spotting these competitive conversational vampires before they drain you dry.

The Classic Moves

The One-Upper is allergic to letting anyone else win. They can't even hear a story without twisting it into an opportunity to remind you that their life has been bigger, better, and more dramatic than yours.

Tell them you got food poisoning once? They've had food poisoning *three times*, from rarer foods, in more exotic locations, and they were still brave enough to go into work the next day. You thought your night of hugging the toilet was bad? They practically survived cholera in the Sahara and lived to tell the tale.

Vacations are a minefield. You say you went to Italy, and they'll cut you off with, "Oh, that's cute—I've *lived* in Italy. I was practically adopted by a vineyard family. Did you even go to Tuscany?

No? Wow." By the end of the conversation, your magical trip to Rome sounds like a weekend in a strip mall.

Family dinners with a One-Upper are guaranteed chaos. You share that your kid just learned to ride a bike. They jump in: "That's adorable. My son was basically training for the Tour de France at that age. He's already broken records. You should really get your kid into sports before it's too late." Congratulations—you're now a failure parent in the eyes of Aunt Karen.

Workplace One-Uppers are equally unbearable. You say, "Man, I worked late last night." They fire back: "Late? I pulled three all-nighters this week, and I'm still crushing it. Some of us are just built different." Translation: they're lying. Nobody works 72 hours straight unless they're in a hostage situation.

Even funerals aren't safe. You quietly share how much you'll miss your grandmother, and the One-Upper swoops in with: "I know how you feel. When *my* grandmother died, it was way harder. She basically raised me, and I was the one who arranged the entire funeral single-handedly while giving a eulogy that made the priest cry." Tragedy Olympics, gold medal.

The worst One-Uppers are the ones who try to disguise it as support. You tell them you finally started going to the gym, and instead of "That's awesome!" you get, "I remember when I started. I was running ten miles a day by week two. Don't worry, you'll get there... maybe." It's not encouragement—it's a slap with a smug grin.

The problem is you can't win against a One-Upper. You can't out-achieve them, because they'll just invent new achievements. They will one-up you on reality, fantasy, and things that haven't even happened yet. You tell them you're getting married, and they'll say, "Oh yeah? I'm already planning my vow renewal for our second honeymoon on a yacht. It's going to be *amazing*."

Conversations with them aren't dialogues—they're contests you never entered. And no matter what the topic is—vacations, jobs, illnesses, traffic jams—they'll always claim the gold medal. Even if they have to fabricate it on the spot.

How to Survive the One-Upper

The bad news: you can't beat a One-Upper. They've been training for this since childhood, fueled by insecurity, caffeine, and the endless need to make every story about them. The good news: you *can* mess with them. Survival isn't about winning—it's about making the game so ridiculous they either run out of steam or, at the very least, move on to irritate someone else.

Here are your tools for endurance:

1. Play Dead

The fastest way to stop feeding their ego is to stop playing altogether. When they start one-upping, don't argue. Don't laugh. Don't even blink. Just stare blankly and nod like you've been lobotomized. They'll hurl story after story at your empty shell until, eventually, they get bored talking to a human paperweight. Bonus: you'll suddenly look mysterious, which they absolutely hate.

2. Out-Ridiculous Them

Fight fire with fireworks. If they say they ran a marathon, you ran two—on your hands, blindfolded, while carrying a small goat. If they brag about a work promotion, you casually mention how you were once CEO of a Fortune 500 company *by accident*. The trick is going so over the top they either realize you're mocking them or they spend three days Googling *"Can you really survive underwater basket weaving in a coal mine?"* Either way, you win.

3. Redirect with Fake Sympathy

Nothing enrages a One-Upper like being treated with pity. The next time they brag about their twelve-hour workday, sigh deeply and say, *"Wow, that sounds... really unhealthy. Have you thought about therapy?"* Watch their face implode as they scramble to pivot from bragging to defending their choices. Delicious.

4. The Sarcastic Clap

When they finish their latest monologue about how they're smarter, faster, fitter, and just generally better than everyone else, give them a slow clap. A real slow clap. Draw it out like you're closing a Broadway show. Throw in a flat, *"Wow, you're amazing."* Even if they don't catch the sarcasm, at least you'll feel like you just booed them off stage.

5. Keep Score

If you're trapped with a chronic One-Upper, turn it into a sport. Bring a notebook and tally points every time they brag. *"Oh, that's your fifth mention of your Tesla today? Five points. At ten, you win a cookie."* They'll either stop to argue about the scoring system or get distracted trying to figure out what the prize is. Pro tip: announce loudly when they hit milestones. "Congratulations, you've hit 20 points! Everyone clap!"

6. Group Sacrifice

Sometimes survival means collateral damage. If you're in a group, casually redirect: *"Hey, didn't Jim just buy a new car?"* Instantly, the One-Upper will pounce, bragging about their own car being faster, shinier, and probably hand-detailed by Beyoncé. Jim suffers, you escape. Sorry, Jim—it was you or me.

7. The Nuclear Option: Agree With Them

The ultimate One-Upper kryptonite is total surrender. When they brag, don't challenge—just say, *"Yep, you're right. You are better. In fact, you might be the best human alive."* The sudden flood of fake validation short-circuits their operating system. They won't know whether to keep bragging or just stand there blinking, crown in hand. Sometimes giving them the throne they're so desperate for is the fastest way to shut them up.

8. Learn to Enjoy the Circus

At some point, you accept the truth: the One-Upper is never going to change. That's when you stop fighting and start enjoying the show. Picture them in full clown makeup, juggling imaginary trophies, honking a horn every time they top your story. It won't make them less annoying, but it will make you laugh. And honestly, laughter is the only real victory.

Final Note: You don't beat a One-Upper. You endure them, out-mock them, or use them as entertainment until they inevitably wander off to find a fresh victim. Just remember survival isn't about topping their stories—it's about topping up your patience (and maybe your wine glass).

The Wrap-Up

The One-Upper is exhausting and relentless. They don't just want to be part of the story—they want to be the story. They can't stand the idea of someone else having a moment, so they swoop in like conversational seagulls, snatching away every crumb of attention you put on the table.

And yet, for all their bluster, they're weirdly fragile. That's the secret nobody tells you. They brag, boast, and inflate because deep down, they can't stand the thought of being ordinary. For them, normal is failure. If you ran a mile, they ran two. If you sprained your ankle, they broke their leg—twice. If you met a celebrity once, they're apparently on a first-name basis with Beyoncé. It's laughable.

The tragedy (and comedy) of the One-Upper is that they think people are impressed. They honestly believe their endless stories make them look cooler, smarter, more successful. In reality, everyone's just nodding, secretly wishing they'd shut up, and mentally drafting texts that say, "Kill me, I'm stuck with Brad again."

And they never stop. Weddings? One-upped. Funerals? One-upped. Baby announcements? Definitely one-upped. There is no sacred ground. You could tell them you got hit by a bus, and they'd respond, "That's crazy—I once got hit by *two* buses, back-to-back, and I still made it to work." You can't win, because they don't play by the rules of reality.

So how do you deal with them? You don't. Not really. You laugh. You roll your eyes. You learn to treat their endless bragging like background noise. Because in the end, the only person they're competing with is themselves. You're not in the race—they just keep dragging you to the starting line.

The real win is stepping back and letting them keep score in a game nobody else is playing. Because when all is said and done, the One-Upper may have the loudest stories, but you'll have the sweetest relief—knowing you don't have to keep pretending that running a 5K while eating a burrito is impressive.

So the next time they puff up and drop their latest humblebrag, just smile, nod, and silently crown them the champion of imaginary victories. Because at the end of the day, the One-Upper always wins—just not in the way they think.

Chapter Five

The Holiday Hunger Games

Holidays are supposed to be about love, gratitude, and togetherness. In reality? They're annual hostage situations with food. You walk in hoping for a peaceful meal, and within fifteen minutes, you're questioning why you didn't just fake the flu and stay home with a frozen pizza.

Let's be clear: family holidays aren't meals. They're war zones with cranberry sauce. They're the Super Bowl of dysfunction. Forget *The Great British Bake Off*—this is *The Great Passive-Aggressive Bake Off,* and you're smack in the middle of it.

It starts the second you walk through the door. The air is thick with stress, perfume that smells like regret, and an unspoken competition over who brought the "best" dish. Aunt Linda's green bean casserole is "just a little dry," Uncle Bob's turkey is "a touch overcooked," and Grandma has already declared that "no one makes pie like she used to." Congratulations, the Hunger Games have begun, may the odds be ever in your favor."

Seating arrangements are strategic combat. You think it's random, but no—every family member knows exactly where they need to sit to maximize drama. Cousins who haven't spoken since the Great Inheritance Argument of 2012 are seated side by side. Someone will get stuck next to the relative who thinks politics is light dinner conversation. And you? You're wedged between the cousin who just discovered CrossFit and the uncle who hasn't stopped chewing since 1985.

Then come the conversations. Or rather, the verbal grenades. The questions are never innocent. "So, when are you getting married?" "Any babies yet?" "Still at that job?" Each one is a landmine, designed to explode on impact. You sip your wine and pray for death, but death doesn't come—just another round of "helpful advice" from people who can't even program their own DVRs.

And don't even get me started on the kitchen. The kitchen is the front line of the Holiday Hunger Games. Passive-aggressive warfare over oven space, whispered criticisms of cooking techniques, and the inevitable shriek of, "Who touched my casserole?!" It's like *Survivor*, but with more butter.

The Moocher (from the last chapter) will be there, naturally, hovering around the buffet like a vulture. The Drama Queen will faint over a burned dinner roll. The Oversharer will give a play-by-play of their rectal examine while you're trying to eat stuffing. The One-Upper will remind you that their turkey last year was juicier, bigger, and probably blessed by Gordon Ramsay. Everyone has a role, and everyone plays it flawlessly.

And the food fights aren't metaphorical. At some point, there will be a real one. Someone will storm off, someone will cry, and someone will dramatically scrape a plate into the trash. By dessert, alliances will have formed, sides will have been chosen, and at least one person will swear they're "never doing this again." Spoiler: they will. Next year. Same time. Same place. Same madness.

Because that's the truth of the Holiday Hunger Games. You hate them, you dread them, you fantasize about skipping them—but deep down, you'd miss them. The chaos, the drama, the backhanded compliments about your haircut—it's all part of the tradition. And like any true warrior, you'll show up again next year, fork in hand because let's be honest, were else do you have to go.

The Classic Moves

The Holiday Hunger Games always follow the same script, no matter whose house you're in. It's like a family Broadway show that never closes—different costumes, same drama, same tears in Act Three.

The Food Fiasco.

There is *always* one dish that causes scandal. It might be undercooked turkey, it might be overcooked turkey, or it might be turkey that looks like it lost a bar fight. Either way, someone will whisper, "Well, it's not how I would've done it," loud enough for everyone within a three-mile radius to hear. Mashed potatoes will be debated like it's a constitutional issue. And God help the poor soul who brought store-bought rolls. That's a family felony.

The Great Table Debate.

No one is ever happy with where they're sitting. If you're single, you get shoved at the kids' table, forced to talk Fortnite with an 11-year-old. If you're married, you get stuck between two relatives who've been arguing about who stole Grandma's china for thirty years. Everyone jockeys for a seat near the pie, but somehow you end up next to Cousin Derek, who chews with his mouth open and talks about cryptocurrency.

The Alcohol Olympics.

Holidays run on booze. That's just science. But the moment the cork pops, the Hunger Games officially begin. Aunt Linda drinks two glasses of wine and suddenly remembers every family feud dating back to 1974. Uncle Bob downs whiskey like it's water and starts telling stories about "the good old days" that absolutely no one asked for. By dessert, someone will be crying, someone will be slurring, and someone will be asleep on the couch with cranberry sauce on their shirt.

The Gift Gauntlet.

If your holiday involves presents, buckle up. The Moocher shows up empty-handed but still expects "something small." The One-Upper hands out gifts that make yours look like trash, while loudly announcing the price tag. Someone inevitably gives an "inside joke" present that stirs up a wound from 1996. And there's always that one relative who "forgot" the gift exchange was happening, even though it's been happening every year since Moses.

The Great Escape Attempts.

By mid-afternoon, half the room is secretly planning their exit. People pretend to "take the dog for a walk" and don't come back for an hour. Teenagers vanish to their rooms. One cousin will claim they have to work tomorrow, even though they're obviously lying. The truly desperate fake food poisoning, which at least buys them a quick getaway.

The Christmas Tree Catastrophe.

If it's a Christmas gathering, something will absolutely happen to the tree. Someone knocks it over. Someone forgets to water it and it bursts into flame. A toddler pulls an ornament and the whole thing comes crashing down. And while everyone scrambles to fix it, the Oversharer starts narrating the disaster like its breaking news.

The truth is that holidays bring out the absolute worst in families—and the best comedy material. These are not peaceful gatherings; they're live-action soap operas where the props just happen to be mashed potatoes and wrapping paper.

How to Survive the Holiday Hunger Games

You can't stop the madness. You can't change your family. You can only survive them—and maybe sneak a little joy while doing it. Think of these less as tips and more as field-tested weapons in the war zone that is holiday dinner.

1. Tactical Wine Refills

Wine isn't just a drink during the holidays—it's camouflage. A full glass signals that you're "busy." Nobody wants to bother someone mid-sip. Keep it topped up at all times. If you don't drink, no problem—fill the glass with grape juice. The key is the illusion.

2. The Bathroom Break Strategy, you have used it before, use it again and again

When tensions rise (and they will), excuse yourself with the most powerful words in the English language: "I need the bathroom." Nobody argues with that. Hide out as long as you need. Scroll your phone, nap, stare into the void—it's all better than listening to Uncle Bob explain cryptocurrency again.

3. Sit Near the Exit

Professional holiday survivors know never sit in the middle of the table. You'll get trapped between relatives, forced to pass dishes like a medieval serf, and unable to escape when the One-Upper starts bragging about their vacation to Bali. Always sit at the edge. Always.

4. Assign Yourself a "Job"

The easiest way to avoid drama? Stay busy. Offer to wash dishes, take out trash or organize leftovers. Everyone else will think you're being helpful, when really, you're running away. Best case scenario, you hide in the kitchen for half the night and only come out when dessert is served.

5. Pie as a Shield

Never underestimate the defensive power of dessert. If someone corners you with political rants or awkward questions, shove a piece of pie in your mouth. You can't answer if you're chewing. If they keep pressing, just keep eating. Eventually, they'll give up or run out of questions.

6. The Fake Call

Technology is your best friend. Set your phone to ring at strategic times. When Aunt Linda starts digging into your love life, gasp dramatically, excuse yourself, and take your "urgent call" in another room. (Bonus: if you really want to sell it, sigh heavily when you return, like you just handled a crisis.)

7. Recruit an Ally

Never go into battle alone. Find your sibling, cousin, or partner—the one who also rolls their eyes at the madness—and form a survival pact. You rescue each other from conversations, swap places at the table, and silently communicate through exaggerated facial expressions.

8. Lower Your Standards

Here's the real trick: stop expecting it to go well. It won't. Accept that there will be arguments, tears, and maybe even a minor fire. Once you embrace the chaos, you stop being disappointed. You might even start laughing at it.

9. Plan a Hard Out

Never arrive without an escape plan. Blame work, the babysitter, the dog—whatever you need. But make it clear you have to leave "by 7." When the turkey takes until 8, you've got a built-in excuse to vanish.

10. Bribe Yourself

Finally, the most important survival tactic: promise yourself a reward. Survive dinner without flipping the table, and you get to binge Netflix, buy yourself something dumb online, or sit in blessed silence with a pint of ice cream.

Because in the end, holidays aren't about joy—they're about survival. And nothing tastes better than freedom after surviving the annual family bloodbath.

Holiday Hunger Games Bingo

Forget peace and joy. Holiday gatherings are basically the Hunger Games with stuffing. Keep this card under the table, and may the odds be ever in your flavor.

Bingo Squares:

Someone cries before dessert.

Passive-aggressive comment about your life choices.

A relative storms off dramatically (bonus if it's over mashed potatoes).

"Back in my day..." monologue.

Two people argue about politics loud enough to scare the dog.

Someone shows up late but still complains the food is cold.

The Moocher takes leftovers "for later."

Drama Queen sighs like a Victorian ghost.

Pet Parent demands everyone clap for Muffin's new sweater.

Someone drops, breaks, or burns something critical.

Awkward toast that reveals way too much.

One-Upper brags about their latest promotion/car/kale cleanse.

Conspiracy Cousin whispers about the turkey being "government controlled."

A kid knocks over a drink onto the good tablecloth.

Someone asks you why you're still single (or when you're having kids).

Bonus Round:

Shout *"BINGO!"* when the fight over board games starts. You'll either get a laugh... or start round two of the Hunger Games.

The Wrap-Up

The Holiday Hunger Games aren't just a meal; they're a ritual. Every family gathers, pretends it's going to be "different this year," and then reenacts the exact same chaos that's been happening since the dawn of time.

The fights? Predictable. The passive-aggressive digs? Guaranteed. The tears? Scheduled right between the salad and dessert. It's like clockwork. You could draw up a bingo card—burned turkey, awkward political rant, someone storming off, somebody "forgetting" to bring what they promised—and you'd win every time before the main course hits the table.

And yet, here's the thing: you'll be back next year. We all will. Because for all the madness, all the guilt-tripping, all the backhanded compliments, holidays give us something else too—stories. Endless, ridiculous, family-lore stories. The kind you'll laugh about later with friends, saying, "You won't believe what happened at Thanksgiving," and they'll respond, "Oh, I believe it. Same here."

So yes, holidays are a circus. Yes, you'll leave stuffed with resentment and mashed potatoes. And yes, you'll swear, "Never again." But deep down, you know the truth: these dysfunctional marathons are what make families... families. Messy, loud, ridiculous, and unforgettable.

So grab your fork, take a deep breath, and enter the arena. May your wine glass be full, your patience slightly less empty, and your pie always within reach. Because in the Holiday Hunger Games, there are no winners—only survivors. And sometimes, survival is the sweetest tradition of all.

CHAPTER SIX

THE GUILT TRIPPER

If Drama Queens thrive on attention and One-Uppers thrive on competition, the Guilt Tripper thrives on misery—*yours*. They don't raise their voices, they don't throw tantrums, and they don't storm out of rooms. No, they wield a far deadlier weapon: passive-aggressive sighs and "disappointed" glances sharp enough to cut steel.

The Guilt Tripper is the emotional pickpocket of the family. You don't even realize what's happening until suddenly you feel bad for not calling, bad for not visiting, bad for not inviting them, bad for not bringing a bigger cake, bad for existing in a way they

THE GUILT TRIPPER 63

didn't pre-approve. You show up thinking you're a functioning adult with free will. You leave questioning whether you're a heartless monster who abandoned your family just because you didn't bring potato salad.

Their greatest skill is subtlety. They won't *say* you're a bad person—they'll just imply it in seventeen different ways until you're begging for forgiveness. "Oh, no, it's fine. We'll just eat alone tonight. Don't worry about us." Translation: *Congratulations, you're a terrible child and probably the reason we can't have nice things.*

Holidays with a Guilt Tripper are psychological boot camps. Everyone else is fighting over gravy; they're quietly dropping landmines like, "I suppose no one wanted to hear about my doctor's appointment." You didn't even know they had an appointment. You didn't ask. But now you feel like you should have hired a marching band to escort them home from it.

The thing about Guilt Trippers is they make you work for their approval like it's a currency. And spoiler: you'll never earn enough. You could send flowers, call every day, visit weekly, and they'd still sigh and say, "Well, it would've been nice if you called *sooner.*" With Guilt Trippers, the glass isn't just half-empty—it's cracked, leaking, and somehow still your fault.

Family Guilt Trippers are the worst because they weaponize love. "After everything I've done for you..." is their battle cry. They raised you, fed you, housed you, clothed you—so naturally, the rest of your life is one long repayment plan. You thought you moved out? Wrong. You're still emotionally paying rent.

And let's not forget the professional-grade martyrdom. No one sacrifices like a Guilt Tripper—at least not in their stories. "Don't worry about me, I'll just sit in the dark." "No, it's fine, I'll take the smaller piece." "Oh, don't get up, I'll clean this entire house myself." Every statement is a trap, designed to make you jump in and rescue them—or live forever with the knowledge that you didn't.

The worst part? It works. Guilt Trippers can squeeze apologies out of stone. They'll make you feel like you've ruined their lives because you couldn't make it to brunch. They're less relatives and more emotional loan sharks, collecting payment in sighs, sad eyes, and backhanded compliments.

So yes, the Drama Queen may drain your energy, and the Moocher may drain your wallet, but the Guilt Tripper? They'll drain your soul—and make you thank them for the privilege.

The Classic Moves

The Guilt Tripper has a weaponized toolkit of tricks, and they know how to use each one with deadly precision. Forget nukes—this is emotional warfare, complete with sighs, eyerolls, and carefully timed pauses designed to crush your spirit.

The Birthday Meltdown. You forget their birthday once—*once*—and you'll never hear the end of it. "Oh, it's fine. I just didn't think anyone remembered me anymore. Not after all the sacrifices I made." You show up the next year with balloons, cake, and a gift basket, and they'll still murmur, "Well, last year was really hard on me." Congratulations, you are now permanently on probation.

The Holiday Hammers. While everyone else is arguing over turkey, the Guilt Tripper is sighing just loudly enough for you to notice. "It's so nice that everyone could make it this year. Well, *almost* everyone." Boom—just like that, Cousin Jenny is crying in the bathroom because she had the audacity to spend Christmas with her in-laws instead.

The "I Guess I'll Die Alone" Classic. If you don't call, if you don't visit, if you don't respond to that random forward they sent at 3 a.m., the Guilt Tripper goes nuclear. "Don't worry about me, I'll just sit here... alone... until the end." Nothing says "family bonding" like being emotionally blackmailed into brunch because your aunt is pretending she's moments away from her obituary.

The Doctor's Appointment Drama. Nothing fuels a Guilt Tripper like a minor health scare. They'll let it slip—strategically—that they went to the doctor, but don't worry, "it's nothing serious." Pause. Pause longer. Wait for the panic to set in. Then comes the dagger: "Of course, no one offered to come with me." Now you're wracked with shame for not dropping everything to accompany them for a cholesterol check.

The Food Martyr Routine. At family dinners, they'll always take the smallest slice, the burnt piece, the plate with less gravy. "Oh no, it's fine—I'll take the leftovers. You all enjoy the good food." Everyone suddenly feels like a greedy monster while they beam, victorious in their self-imposed starvation.

The Gift Exchange Guilt-Bomb. You buy them something nice, but not extravagant enough, and the sigh begins. "Oh, you didn't have to get me anything." Translation: you should've gotten them more. Next year, you overcompensate with something expensive, and they hit you with, "Oh dear, you really shouldn't have spent so much." With Guilt Trippers, it's never about the gift—it's about making sure you feel terrible no matter what.

The Parent Trap. Parents who guilt trip are in a league of their own. "I changed your diapers, and this is how you repay me?" or "After everything I gave up for you, you can't even visit once a week?" You could buy them a house, and they'd still sigh about how you never call enough. With parent Guilt Trippers, life is basically an eternal punishment for being born.

The beauty of the Guilt Tripper's technique is that they never attack directly. No yelling, no cursing, no throwing plates. Just carefully engineered phrases that stick in your brain like gum on a shoe. You'll lie awake at night replaying their words, wondering if you really are the selfish monster they've painted you to be. Spoiler: you're not—it's just their full-time job to make you feel that way.

How to Survive the Guilt Tripper

You can't stop a Guilt Tripper from guilt-tripping. It's not a phase; it's their life's purpose. But you *can* stop them from ruining yours. Here's how.

1. Build Guilt-Proof Armor

Think of guilt like emotional acid rain—it only burns if it lands. You've got to coat yourself in mental Teflon. Every sigh, every "It's fine, don't worry about me," every "I guess I'll just eat alone," just bounces off. Practice repeating this mantra: *"Their guilt is not my homework."* Because that's exactly what it is—they're assigning you emotional essays you didn't sign up to write.

2. Deploy the Silent Stare

When they launch into a guilt trip, don't defend yourself. Don't explain. Just stare at them. Calm, unblinking, blank face. Let them marinate in their own drama. Nothing unnerves a Guilt Tripper like not knowing if their manipulation landed.

3. Pretend to Misunderstand

"Oh, you mean you *want* me to call more? I thought you enjoyed your alone time!" Play dumb. Weaponize cluelessness. Guilt Trippers rely on you "getting it." If you act like you don't, they short-circuit. Suddenly, they're the one over-explaining, and you get to sip your wine in peace.

4. Call Their Bluff

The Guilt Tripper thrives on theatrics. Test them. The next time they say, "I guess I'll just sit here in the dark," offer to buy them a flashlight. When they sigh, "I suppose I'll just eat whatever's left," hand them the burnt roll. Watch them deflate like a sad balloon.

5. Keep Receipts

Literally, keep receipts. Guilt Trippers will claim you "never do anything for them." Bust out the list: the calls, the visits, the favors. "Funny, because I actually came over three times last week, fixed your Wi-Fi, and brought lasagna." There's no better feeling than guilt-tripping the Guilt Tripper.

6. Use the "Yes, And" Trick

It's an improv technique, but deadly in guilt warfare. They say, "After everything I've done for you..." You reply, "Yes, and after everything I've done for you, I think we're even." Boom. Checkmate.

7. Say "No" Without a Sermon

The most terrifying word in the Guilt Tripper dictionary? No. Say it. Practice it. Deliver it without a long explanation. The less you justify, the less room they have to twist your words into more guilt. You'll feel like you've just survived a bungee jump, but the power rush is worth it.

8. Reward Good Behavior (Like They're a Dog)

Every once in a while, the Guilt Tripper might ask for something *without* layering on the shame. Reward them. Positive reinforcement works wonders. A little "Thank you for just asking directly" can sometimes retrain them—if only for five glorious minutes.

The Wrap-Up

The Guilt Tripper is proof that you don't need volume to control a room. No shouting, no tantrums—just sighs, side-eyes, and those lethal one-liners that stick in your head long after dinner's over. They're emotional ninjas, slicing you to ribbons with whispers and "Don't worry about me" bombs.

And if you've ever thought, *Maybe I'm imagining it, maybe they're not that bad,* let me assure you: you're not imagining it. I once had a Guilt Tripper aunt who could have won medals. I forgot to call her one Easter. Just once. The next time I saw her, she greeted me with, "Well, well, look who's still alive." That was her hello. Not "How are you?" Not "Good to see you." Just an emotional shiv right between the ribs. I spent the entire dinner overcompensating—refilling her wine, complimenting her sweater, even offering to do dishes—like some penitent servant repaying a debt. She never thanked me. She just sighed and said, "It's the least you could do." Reader, I nearly lit myself on fire in the yard.

That's the Guilt Tripper magic: you end up apologizing for things you didn't even do. You start rearranging your life to avoid their disapproval. They've got you running emotional errands you never signed up for, and they're collecting payment with interest.

But here's the secret: guilt only works if you let it. Guilt is a hook, and the Guilt Tripper is dangling it like bait. Once you learn not to bite—once you laugh at the sighs instead of swallowing them—they lose their power. They can't guilt you into calls, visits, or casseroles if you stop buying into the performance.

Because the truth is, Guilt Trippers will always be disappointed. That's their default setting. If you call daily, they'll wish you called twice. If you visit weekly, they'll want daily. If you sacrifice everything, they'll still find a way to sigh. So why bother? The only winning move is to stop playing the game.

So the next time they drop their famous line—"Don't worry about me, I'll be fine"—smile, say "Great!" and walk away. Watch their face crumble as you leave them holding their own empty guilt balloon. It's glorious. It's liberating. And it's the only way to survive the emotional tax collectors of family life.

CHAPTER SEVEN
THE DRUCK UNCLE

Every family has a Drunk Uncle. He may not technically be your uncle—sometimes he's a cousin, sometimes he's a family friend, sometimes he's a guy nobody remembers inviting—but he's always *there*. And you know he's arrived before he even walks in the door, because you can hear him in the driveway, laughing at his own jokes like he just won a comedy special.

The Drunk Uncle is the human equivalent of a half-empty beer can: loud, sloppy, and questionable to hold. He shows up late, already "a little buzzed," and immediately announces, "The party can start now!" Translation: the party was fine until he got there, and now everyone is bracing for disaster.

He's a walking cocktail of bad habits. He drinks too much, too fast, and too often—and he thinks it makes him charming. In reality, it makes him sweaty, red-faced, and just a little too handsy. He believes every burp is hilarious, every story is fascinating, and every woman in the room secretly wants him. Spoiler: they don't. They want him to sit down, shut up, and stop winking at the waitstaff.

Conversation with the Drunk Uncle is a game of roulette. You never know which version you're going to get. Sometimes he's the "fun uncle," telling exaggerated stories about his glory days in high school sports, even though no one remembers him making the team. Sometimes he's the "philosophical uncle," slurring his way through a rant about politics, the economy, or how kids "don't respect hard work anymore." And sometimes he's the "creepy uncle," hovering a little too close, laughing a little too long, and complimenting someone half his age in a way that makes everyone check where the exits are.

The Drunk Uncle's timing is impeccable—in the worst way. He'll say the most inappropriate thing possible at the exact wrong moment. A heartfelt toast? He interrupts with a belch and a story about his ex-wife. A family photo? He's in the back, flashing devil horns and holding a beer like it's a newborn child. A quiet dinner prayer? He's whispering to the person next to him about how he once "almost met Bon Jovi."

And God forbid someone tries to cut him off. The Drunk Uncle treats bartenders like villains and family members like prison guards. "What, I can't have *one more*?" he'll whine, holding his eighth drink. "Come on, I'm just having fun!" His definition of fun usually involves knocking over something expensive, falling asleep on the couch with one shoe on, and accidentally trauma-tizing a child with an off-color story.

The worst part? He thinks he's the life of the party. He thinks everyone is laughing *with* him, when really, they're laughing *at* him—or pretending to laugh so he doesn't start a scene. The Drunk Uncle lives in a bubble of booze-fueled confidence, con-vinced he's the funniest, smartest, most handsome man in the room. In reality, he's the cautionary tale parents whisper to their kids: *Don't end up like Uncle Steve.*

But here's the kicker: despite all the chaos, despite the cringe, despite the fact that he once tried to slow dance with the Christ-mas tree, the Drunk Uncle always gets invited back. Because deep down, every family knows the truth: without him, the holiday chaos wouldn't feel complete. He's the disaster you dread, the cringe you can't escape, and the story you'll retell for years.

The Classic Moves

The Drunk Uncle doesn't just drink—he performs. Every sip is a warm-up act for the chaos to come. And no matter how many times he's done it, every family gathering plays out the same way: like a Broadway show nobody wanted tickets to.

The Karaoke Incident. If there's music—*any* music—the Drunk Uncle will try to sing. Doesn't matter if it's Christmas carols, happy birthday, or the hold music on your mom's speak-erphone—he's got the mic, and he's not letting go. He belts out off-key renditions of Bon Jovi or Billy Joel, swaying with the grace of a collapsing filing cabinet. And when the applause doesn't come, he just claps for himself.

The Hug That Lasts Too Long. The Drunk Uncle doesn't respect personal space. Hugs aren't just hugs—they're full-body, slightly sweaty embraces that last a beat too long. Add in a whispered "You've always been my favorite" and suddenly you need a Silkwood shower.

The Over-Sharer's Evil Twin. He's the drunk version of the Oversharer, armed with a six-pack and zero boundaries. Within twenty minutes he's telling the kids about "that one wild night in Vegas" and the adults about his colonoscopy. Both stories have way too much detail, and both will scar you for life.

The Creepy Compliments. One of the most predictable (and cringiest) parts of the Drunk Uncle routine is the moment he decides he's irresistible. He'll wink at your friends, flirt with the waitress, and announce, "Hey, I've still got it!" Spoiler: he doesn't. He lost it somewhere around 1998.

The Nap Attack. Inevitably, the Drunk Uncle will pass out in the middle of the action. Sometimes it's on the couch, sometimes it's in a chair, sometimes it's face-down in the mashed potatoes. Wherever it happens, it's never subtle. There will be snoring. There will be drooling. And there will be at least one photo circulated on Facebook within the hour.

The Angry Turn. Booze roulette always has one dark side. One second, he's "funny drunk uncle," the next, he's red-faced and ranting about politics, taxes, or how "kids today don't appreciate anything." He slams his beer on the table, knocks something over, and storms out—before stumbling back in ten minutes later like nothing happened.

The Christmas Tree Massacre. Every family with a Drunk Uncle has a story about the year he took out the Christmas tree.

Maybe he tripped over the cord, maybe he tried to dance with it, maybe he just leaned a little too hard—but down it went, ornaments shattering like tiny bombs. He laughed, everyone else cried, and it became family lore forever.

The Drunk Uncle is chaos wrapped in a beer-stained flannel. You don't invite him for entertainment value—you invite him because you know he's inevitable. He's the family hurricane. He's the walking hangover. He's the man who proves, year after year, that alcohol and "dad jokes" should never mix.

How to Survive the Drunk Uncle

You can't ban him. You can't sober him up. You can't reason with him. The Drunk Uncle is like glitter—once he's in the room, you're stuck with him until long after the party's over. The only option is survival. Think of it as storm prep: stock up, know your exits, and pray the karaoke machine breaks.

1. Hide the Good Booze

This one's simple: stash the expensive wine, the fancy whiskey, and anything you don't want contaminated by backwash. Leave out the cheap beer. He won't notice. He's not here for tasting notes—he's here for volume. Bonus: you'll avoid the inevitable *"Lemme just top you off"* pour that's 90% Uncle, 10% actual alcohol.

2. Control the Seating Chart

Strategic placement is everything. Keep him far away from the kids, the fragile heirlooms, and the friend he's inevitably going to hit on. Ideally, seat him between Cousin Derek (who's half deaf) and Grandma (who's asleep by dessert). The Drunk Uncle thrives on an audience—remove that, and he's just a man yelling at a gravy boat.

3. Master the Irish Goodbye

When the Drunk Uncle corners you, escape is the only option. No long goodbyes. No excuses. Just vanish. Slip into the kitchen, the garage, or the neighbor's yard if necessary. By the time he realizes you're gone, he'll be halfway through his "high school glory days" story, telling it to a lamp.

4. Have a Decoy Topic Ready

Keep distraction grenades at the ready. Too loud? Too creepy? Too political? Drop a phrase like:

"Did you see the game last night?"

"What do you think about gas prices?"

"Weren't you in the Navy?"

Instantly, he's off on a rant, and you're free. Warning: do not use religion, cryptocurrency, or "the neighbor's new car" unless you're prepared for a three-hour filibuster.

5. Stage a Fake Intervention

Advanced move. Gather two relatives, put on your best serious faces, and whisper: *"Uncle Steve, we really need to talk."* Lead him to a quiet room... and leave him there. He'll spend the next half hour pacing, wondering what he did wrong (answer: everything). That's 30 glorious minutes of freedom for everyone else.

6. Use the Power of Nap Time

Lean into the inevitable. After his fifth beer, gently guide him toward the couch. Toss a blanket over him, dim the lights, and let him snore like a chainsaw. Congratulations, you've defused the bomb—at least until he wakes up at 2 a.m. demanding pie and/or starting round two.

7. Weaponize Shame-by-Photo

The Drunk Uncle thrives on believing he's charming. Kill the illusion. Snap photos of his karaoke, his weird dance moves, or his turkey-face-down nap. The next morning, casually drop them into the family group chat. He'll deny, he'll deflect, but nothing pierces his armor faster than seeing himself half-naked doing "the worm."

8. Accept That He's Part of the Circus

Here's the truth: the Drunk Uncle is tradition. He's been falling into punch bowls, creeping out your friends, and embarrassing himself since before you were born. You're not going to fix him. What you *can* do is laugh, roll your eyes, and add his latest disaster to the family highlight reel. Because in ten years, nobody will remember the perfectly roasted turkey—but everyone will remember the time Uncle Dan tried to fistfight the inflatable Santa on the front lawn.

Drunk Uncle Bingo

Every family has one. He's part comedian, part philosopher, part HR violation. Play along at your next holiday dinner — but don't expect to finish a square without wincing.

Bingo Squares:

Falls asleep in the recliner mid-sentence.

Starts a story with *"Back in my day..."* and never finishes it.

Makes wildly inappropriate toast.

Brings up politics at the worst possible time.

Calls someone by the wrong name (bonus: it's a relative he's known for 20 years).

Spills drink on the tablecloth.

Retells the same story three times in one night.

Tries to wrestle with a nephew or son-in-law.

Belts out karaoke with no music playing.

Refers to shots as "hydration."

Slurs through a conspiracy theory.

Volunteers to carve the turkey... and should not be trusted with knives.

Tells a joke that ends with *"That's what she said."*

Argues with someone who isn't actually arguing back.

Needs to be "walked" to the Uber.

Bonus Square:

Yell *"Bingo!"* if he takes off his shirt to "prove a point."

The Wrap-Up

The Drunk Uncle is a guaranteed disaster wrapped in flannel and beer breath. He's the man, the myth, the legend who will *always* be inappropriate at the exact wrong moment. He doesn't just cross lines—he trips over them, spills beer on them, and then insists the line was never there in the first place.

And the funniest part? He thinks he's charming. He believes his jokes are hilarious, his dance moves are impressive, and his stories are epic. In reality, the only thing epic is the family-wide eye roll that greets him the second he walks in. He's not the star of the show—he's the blooper reel no one can turn off.

I once watched a Drunk Uncle (let's call him "Uncle Bob" because of course his name was Bob) attempt to lead a toast. By "toast," I mean he stood up on a chair, sloshed beer onto the tablecloth, and started singing "Sweet Caroline." No one joined in.

Not one person. By the time he got to "ba ba baaa," he'd already lost his balance and taken down half the centerpiece. My grandma just muttered, "This is why we can't have nice things," while the rest of us applauded—not for the toast, but for the fact that the chair didn't break under him.

That's the thing about Drunk Uncles: they're predictable in the most unpredictable way. You never know if tonight's performance will involve karaoke, accidental nudity, or a drunken lecture about "how women used to know their place." But you do know one thing—you'll be telling the story for years.

So yes, he's creepy. Yes, he's exhausting. Yes, you'll dread sitting next to him. But he's also a reminder that family dysfunction isn't tidy—it's loud, messy, and sometimes face-down in the mashed potatoes. And honestly? If he ever cleaned up his act, you'd almost miss the chaos. Almost.

CHAPTER EIGHT
THE TOXIC FRIEND

We all have that one friend. The one who drains your energy, tests your patience, and somehow convinces you it's your fault. You know the type—the *Toxic Friend*. They're less a friend and more an emotional parasite, but for some reason, you keep answering their texts like they're offering free pizza instead of free misery.

The Toxic Friend is a master of disguise. Sometimes they show up as the "fun one," dragging you into wild nights that always end with you holding their hair back over a toilet. Sometimes they're the "needy one," guilt-tripping you into constant emotional labor, as if you're their personal 24/7 therapist. And sometimes they're the "competitive one," secretly rooting for you to fail so they can feel better about their own trainwreck of a life. No matter which mask they wear, the result is the same: you leave every interaction feeling exhausted, annoyed, or strangely guilty.

Conversations with the Toxic Friend are like emotional quicksand—you step in thinking it's safe, and before you know it, you're sinking under the weight of their problems, their drama, their endless chaos. You can't win. If you give advice, they ignore it. If you don't give advice, you're "unsupportive." If you dare to talk about *your* life, they pivot the spotlight back to themselves faster than a Broadway diva on opening night.

And let's not forget their uncanny ability to sabotage. Big date? They'll call crying about their latest breakup. Job interview? They'll text you a crisis right before you leave the house. Vacation? They'll tag you in some cryptic Facebook post designed to guilt you for "having fun while others are suffering." Somehow, your good news always triggers their bad news, and suddenly you're back in the role of their unpaid life coach.

The Toxic Friend also has a PhD in double standards. They'll vanish when you need them most, but the second they stub their toe, they expect you to drop everything and rush to their side. They'll ghost you for weeks, then explode if you don't reply to their 2 a.m. meltdown texts within three minutes. Loyalty, in their mind, is a one-way street—with them in the driver's seat, flooring it, while you cling to the roof rack.

And here's the kicker: they don't even realize they're toxic. In their mind, they're just "being real" or "telling it like it is." They think their constant criticism is "helpful," their sabotage is "protective," and their endless drama is "just how friendship works."

Meanwhile, you're quietly Googling "how to fake your own death to get out of plans."

The worst part? Cutting off a Toxic Friend feels harder than breaking up with a partner. Families expect you to tolerate annoying relatives, but friends are supposed to be chosen. So why do we keep choosing these disasters? Maybe it's nostalgia. Maybe it's guilt. Or maybe we've just been gaslit into believing that enduring their nonsense is the price of admission for friendship.

But let's be real: friendship isn't supposed to feel like an unpaid internship in emotional labor. If every time you see their name on your phone, your soul whispers "oh no," congratulations—you've got a Toxic Friend.

The Classic Moves

Toxic Friends aren't content with being mildly annoying. No, they thrive on chaos. They don't just trip you up; they build a whole obstacle course and then act shocked when you stumble.

The Saboteur. The Toxic Friend has an instinct for ruining milestones. Got a date? They'll text you a five-paragraph essay about their heartbreak as you're walking out the door. Nail an interview? They'll call crying because their cat "looked at them weird." Planning a vacation? They'll suddenly remember a traumatic event from 15 years ago that only you can "help them process" *right now*.

The Fake Cheerleader. On the surface, they'll clap for your wins. But the applause is always laced with venom. You say, "I got promoted!" and they go, "Wow, that's great—for someone with no experience." You announce you're moving into a new apartment, and they mutter, "Must be nice to afford rent without your parents' help." Backhanded compliments are their Olympic sport, and they're undefeated.

The Black Hole of Energy. Spend ten minutes with them and you'll feel like you've run a marathon. Every conversation is about their problems, their drama, their exes, their "enemies." It's like emotional cardio—except instead of losing weight, you lose willpower. You hang up the phone needing a nap, a drink, and maybe an exorcism.

The Guilt-Bomb Texts. Toxic Friends are famous for sending messages that sound like threats wrapped in emojis. "I guess you're too busy for me." "Don't worry, I'll figure it out... alone." "Hope you're having fun while I'm suffering." Every ping from them is a tiny grenade of guilt waiting to blow up your day.

The Emergency Factory. Nobody manufactures crises like a Toxic Friend. They're late for work? Emergency. They lost their keys? Emergency. They can't find their left sock? Catastrophe. Meanwhile, when you're facing a genuine problem—like, say, your car catching fire—they're too busy posting cryptic quotes on Instagram.

The Jealous Shadow. The moment you make a new friend, the Toxic Friend goes full detective. "So... who were you with? Why didn't you invite me? Do they make you laugh more than I do?" It's not friendship—it's custody. They want full control of your time, your energy, and your social life.

The Walking Contradiction. They'll ghost you for three weeks, then rage when you don't answer their text in three minutes. They'll trash talk your other friends, then wonder why no one invites them anywhere. They'll borrow money, clothes, or Netflix passwords, then act offended if you even hint at wanting them back.

The worst part? They always circle back. No matter how many times you distance yourself, no matter how many boundaries you try to set, Toxic Friends have the persistence of cockroaches. Block them today, and they'll pop up tomorrow with a cheery "Hey bestie, miss youuu!" as if they didn't just emotionally drain you like a leech with Wi-Fi access.

How to Survive the Toxic Friend

Escaping a Toxic Friend isn't easy. They cling harder than a toddler at daycare drop-off. But with the right strategies, you can keep your sanity—and maybe even your Netflix password.

1. Master the "Phone Battery Death"

The oldest trick in the book. When the texts start rolling in—"Why didn't you answer? Are you mad at me? Do you still care about me?"—just let your phone *die*. No explanation needed. You're not ignoring them; you're simply a victim of technology. Bonus points if you occasionally sprinkle in a "Sorry! Phone died again!" for believability.

2. Deploy the Emotional Hazmat Suit

Picture yourself in full protective gear every time they call. Their drama bounces off like toxic waste on rubber. The sighs, the guilt trips, the endless monologues about Chad who ghosted them for the 17th time—it all rolls right off. Smile, nod, and repeat this sacred mantra: *"Not my circus, not my monkeys."*

3. Ghosting, But Make It Casual

You don't have to vanish completely (though tempting). Start small. Take longer to reply. "Forget" to like their posts. Pretend you're busy binge-watching an obscure 12-season show. Slowly starve them of attention until they latch onto someone else's energy supply.

4. Weaponize Fake Enthusiasm

If you can't escape, overwhelm them. Whenever they share their latest drama, respond with over-the-top cheerleading. "Oh my gosh, Chad ghosted you AGAIN? That's AMAZING, you're like breaking records!" Sarcasm sails over their head, but the sheer weirdness might scare them off.

5. Keep Conversations on a Timer

Set a limit—ten minutes max. When the clock runs out, end the call with a fake emergency. "Oh no, the oven's on fire!" "My dog just learned how to drive, gotta go!" Any excuse will do. They'll barely notice—they're too busy talking about themselves to process what you said.

6. Introduce Them to Another Toxic Friend

It's risky, but brilliant. Pair two Toxic Friends together. They'll cancel each other out, locked in a never-ending competition of who's suffering more. It's like throwing two dementors into the same room and letting them duke it out.

7. Say "No" Without the Novel

Toxic Friends thrive on loopholes. If you explain too much, they'll find a way back in. Keep it short. Keep it blunt. "No, I can't." That's it. No "maybe later," no "if I'm free," no "I'll try." Just *no*. It'll sting, but like ripping off a band-aid, it's fast, clean, and surprisingly satisfying.

8. Schedule Them Like a Dentist Appointment

If you insist on keeping them around, limit their access. Book them like you'd book a root canal—strictly scheduled, carefully contained, and definitely not too often. That way, you know exactly when the pain is coming and can mentally prepare with snacks, alcohol, or noise-canceling headphones.

9. Consider Witness Protection

When all else fails, fake your own death. Okay, maybe that's dramatic, but disappearing to another city with a new name suddenly doesn't sound so bad after the sixth midnight meltdown call in a row.

The Wrap-Up

The Toxic Friend is proof that not all bad relationships wear a romantic label. Some of them hide under the word *friendship*, sucking the life out of you one backhanded compliment at a time. They don't yell, they don't break up with you, and they don't move away. They just linger—like a bad smell in the fridge you can't quite locate.

They're always "there for you," but in the way mold is "there" for bread. They call it loyalty. You call it emotional exhaustion. And no matter how many times you try to step back, they reappear with a dramatic, "Miss you, bestie!" as if the last six months of manipulation were just a quirky personality trait.

I had one Toxic Friend in college who could've written the manual. She'd call me every night, usually at 1 a.m., crying about how "nobody cares about her." I'd stay up, half-asleep, coaching her through another made-up catastrophe. The next day, I'd find out she was mad at me because I didn't *sound enthusiastic enough* during her meltdown. The kicker? When I went through my own actual crisis—job loss, rent overdue, life in shambles—her response was, "That sucks. Anyway, let me tell you about *my* week." Reader, I nearly threw my Nokia through a wall.

That's the Toxic Friend experience in a nutshell: you give, they take. You listen, they talk. You support, they drain. And at the end of it, you're left wondering why you're more exhausted after a "catch-up coffee" than after running a 10K.

But here's the thing—they only win if you let them. Once you realize that friendship isn't a hostage situation, you take your power back. You stop answering every call. You stop bending over backward. You start saying no—and you notice something magical: the weight lifts. The air clears. And you finally remember what it feels like to have friends who don't make you want to fake your own funeral.

So the next time the Toxic Friend slides into your DMs with a casual, "We need to talk," take a deep breath, smile, and say the most liberating word in the English language: *No.* They'll live. You'll thrive. And for once, you'll leave a friendship feeling lighter, not drained.

CHAPTER NINE
THE IN-LAW OLYMPICS

Marrying into a family doesn't just mean you get a spouse—it means you get a front-row seat to the circus that raised them. Congratulations: you didn't just say "I do" to your partner, you said "I do" to their entire dysfunctional family tree. And the branch with the sharpest thorns? The in-laws.

Dealing with in-laws isn't an activity. It's a sport. A grueling, year-round competition where the medals are emotional exhaustion, forced smiles, and casserole-induced bloating. Welcome to the In-Law Olympics, where every holiday, barbecue, and casual Sunday dinner is a high-stakes event.

The Opening Ceremony begins the second you step into their house. Judging eyes scan your outfit. Someone makes a comment about how you "don't eat much" or "went back for seconds." The passive-aggressive commentary flows like wine—"We always did things *this* way," "That's not how we usually make it," "Oh, we never used to talk like that in this family." And there you are, balancing a paper plate on your lap like a contestant in some humiliating endurance game show.

In-laws love to compete for dominance. The mother-in-law usually leads the pack, wielding passive-aggression like an Olympic torch. Her specialty event? The Backhanded Compliment Marathon. "What a lovely dress—it must be so forgiving on your figure." The father-in-law, meanwhile, excels in the "Let Me Give You Unsolicited Financial Advice" sprint. He'll corner you in the kitchen to explain how you're "doing retirement all wrong," even though he's still paying off three boats.

Then there are the siblings-in-law. Oh, the siblings. You thought you were marrying one person—you didn't realize you were signing up for a lifelong rivalry with people who still bring up who got the bigger slice of cake at age six. They'll compare jobs, kids, houses, vacations, even who brought the better dip to the barbecue. You could cure cancer and they'd still find a way to one-up you: "Oh, wow, that's nice, but Becky ran a 5K last weekend."

And let's not forget the relatives who've decided you're "not really family." These are the referees of the In-Law Olympics, constantly reminding you that no matter how long you've been married, you'll always be the outsider. You'll always be "the one who married in." Like you're a contestant on *Survivor* waiting to see if you get voted off the island before dessert.

Family traditions are the main event. God help you if you suggest changing one. "We *always* have ham on Christmas." "We *always* open presents at midnight." "We *always* burn the turkey and pretend it's fine." Break tradition, and you're out of the competition. Forever.

And of course, the commentary never stops. Everything you do is scored. The way you cook, the way you parent, the way you breathe—it's all up for critique. You're not just living your life; you're performing in front of judges who never asked you to audition. And the worst part? The scoring system is rigged. No matter how hard you try, you'll always be "almost" good enough.

So yes, marriage gives you love, partnership, and companionship—but it also gives you the In-Law Olympics. And once you're in, there's no tapping out. You're competing for life.

Classic Moves

If in-laws were an Olympic team, their events would look something like this:

The Casserole Competition. Every family gathering includes at least three versions of the same dish, all presented as if they belong in a museum. You politely compliment one, and suddenly you've started World War III in the kitchen. "Oh, so you liked *her* casserole better?" Congratulations, you've just scored a perfect 10 in Unintentional Offense.

The Gift-Giving Gauntlet. Forget joy—this is about strategy. If you spend too much, you're "showing off." Too little, you're "thoughtless." And God help you if you buy a gift card. That's not a gift, it's a felony. By the end, everyone's fake smiling through clenched teeth, wondering who secretly kept the receipt.

The Parenting Pentathlon. If you have kids, buckle up. In-laws never miss an opportunity to critique your parenting. "We didn't use car seats back then." "Screens will rot their brains." "Back in my day, we spanked them, and they turned out fine." (No, they didn't. Look at Uncle Bob.) It's a constant game of defense, where every juice box and bedtime is judged like you're on trial at The Hague.

The Silent Treatment Relay. Nothing says "family bonding" like an in-law storming off mid-conversation, only to return later acting like nothing happened. The baton in this event is resentment, and it gets passed down through generations.

The Financial Advice Sprint. Father-in-law corners you with unsolicited money wisdom: "What you need to do is buy property." "Have you looked at crypto?" "Back when I was your age, I already owned three houses." The irony? He's currently paying off a timeshare in Florida and driving a car held together by duct tape.

The Passive-Aggressive Decathlon. This isn't one event—it's ten. From side comments about your cooking to digs about how you "don't call enough," every remark is a carefully sharpened dart disguised as small talk. You leave with a stomach full of pie and a head full of shame.

The Exit Drama Sprint. Just when you think you've survived, someone has to leave dramatically. They slam the door, mutter something about being "unappreciated," and peel out of the driveway. Five minutes later, your spouse is on the phone begging them to come back next year.

The truth is, the In-Law Olympics aren't about fun—they're about survival. The judges are biased, the rules change constantly, and no matter how hard you compete, you'll never take home the gold. At best, you'll stumble away clutching a participation ribbon that says: *Congratulations, you made it through dinner without crying in the bathroom.*

How to Survive the In-Law Olympics

You can't win the In-Law Olympics. The scoring is rigged, the judges are corrupt, and the medal ceremony always ends with tears. But with the right strategy, you can make it through without losing your sanity—or your marriage.

1. Perfect the Olympic Smile

This isn't your real smile. This is the smile you practice in the mirror, the one that says: *I hear your passive-aggressive insult, and I choose peace because I like sleeping in my own bed.* Wear it like armor. No matter what they say about your cooking, your clothes, or your life choices—smile. A tight, terrifying smile.

2. Learn the Sacred Phrase: "That's Interesting."

Nothing shuts down an in-law rant faster than a neutral response. "That's interesting" is the duct tape of family conversations. They tell you your parenting is all wrong? "That's interesting." They explain why your job isn't a "real career"? "That's interesting." Translation: *Kindly shut up before I stab myself with a fork.*

3. Develop Secret Signals With Your Spouse

You need a covert language. A raised eyebrow means "rescue me." A squeeze of the hand means "change the subject." A gentle kick under the table means "I swear to God, if your mother comments on my weight again, we're leaving." Think of it as Morse code for marital survival.

4. Use the Bathroom Strategy

If it worked for dodging the Guilt Tripper, it'll work here too. Long bathroom breaks are the perfect escape. Nobody questions them, and the solitude is pure bliss. Bring your phone, scroll Instagram, breathe. Those ten stolen minutes might be the highlight of the entire evening.

5. Create Fake Appointments

Plan your exit before you even arrive. "We'd love to stay, but we have to get going—dog sitter, early morning, house inspection, alien abduction, you name it." The excuse doesn't matter. What matters is that you get to leave before dessert turns into another round of family drama.

6. Master the Art of Strategic Forgetfulness

"Oh no, I must've forgotten the recipe you wanted." "Oops, I completely spaced on calling about that thing." Pretend to be forgetful when the requests pile up. In-laws expect you to remember everything. Forgetting is self-defense.

7. Build an Ally

Find the one sane person in the room. Maybe it's your spouse's cousin, maybe it's Grandma after her third sherry. Team up. Make snide comments under your breath, roll your eyes in unison, and laugh at the madness together. Surviving the In-Law Olympics is easier in pairs.

8. Pick Your Battles (Hint: Pick None)

Want to win an argument with your in-laws? You can't. They have decades of experience and no shame. It's like trying to out-swim a dolphin—you'll drown before you get close. Smile, nod, and save your energy for the car ride home, where you can rant freely with your spouse.

9. Keep a Secret Snack Stash

Because sometimes, the only comfort is chocolate. When the stress hits, sneak away to the pantry and eat your contraband like you're hiding from a bear. Survival isn't pretty, but it's delicious.

In-Law Olympics Bingo

Every marriage comes with bonus relatives, and every gathering turns into a full-contact sport. Keep this card handy the next time you're drafted into competition. May the odds be ever in your casserole's favor.

Bingo Squares:

Backhanded compliment about your cooking.

"When are you having kids?" interrogation.

Critique of your house/car/clothes/face.

Unsolicited parenting advice.

Passive-aggressive comment about your job.

Someone "helpfully" rearranges your kitchen.

In-law shows up with a "better" version of the dish you made.

Silent judgmental stare that lasts more than 10 seconds.

Story about how your partner "used to date someone better."

Casual mention of family gossip you weren't supposed to hear.

Financial advice you didn't ask for.

Comparison to another sibling/cousin (*"Well, Jessica just bought a house…"*).

Someone asks if you've "put on weight" (bonus: in front of the whole table).

Reminder of "the way we do things in this family."

Wine mysteriously topped up... past safe levels.

Bonus Square:

Stand up and yell *"Gold medal!"* if your casserole survives without being critiqued. (Spoiler: it won't.)

The Wrap-Up

The In-Law Olympics aren't about love, family, or tradition—they're about endurance. You don't "win." You survive. And if you make it to the closing ceremony without crying in the bathroom, snapping at someone's backhanded compliment, or chugging wine straight from the bottle, you've already earned the gold.

In-laws thrive on subtle warfare: the raised eyebrows, the sighs, the unsolicited advice about things they barely understand. Every gathering is just another competition, another event where you're being judged, scored, and found slightly lacking. The trick isn't to fight—it's to laugh. Treat their digs like commentary from bad sports announcers. *"And there it is, another jab at the stuffing consistency. Truly groundbreaking criticism from a woman who burns water."*

I once spent Christmas at my in-laws where the turkey carving became an Olympic event all on its own. My father-in-law gave a 45-minute commentary on how I was "holding the knife wrong." By the end, half the turkey was shredded, everyone was starving, and I was ready to stab myself with the carving fork just to end the play-by-play. Did anyone thank me for my efforts? No. But did I win? Also no. The winner was my mother-in-law, who got to say, "See, I told you he'd make a mess." Bravo. Gold medal secured.

That's the reality of the In-Law Olympics—you'll never beat them at their own games. The judging panel is biased, the scoring system changes mid-round, and the competition never ends. But the secret victory is walking out the door with your sanity (mostly) intact, your spouse still on your side, and your sense of humor sharpened like a sword.

So, when the in-laws hand you your participation ribbon—disguised as another dig about how you "don't visit enough"—smile, wave, and tuck it in your pocket. You survived the games. And sometimes, survival is all you need.

Chapter Ten
The Social Media Show-Off

You know that one relative or friend who can't eat a sandwich without posting about it? The one who documents their life like they're auditioning for a reality show no one asked to watch? Congratulations, you've met the Social Media Show-Off.

They're not just online—they *live* online. Every family dinner, holiday, and casual gathering is an unpaid photoshoot. Forget enjoying the moment—you're just a background extra in their never-ending quest for likes. You thought you were coming over for dinner? Wrong. You're here to be tagged in a blurry group shot captioned "Fam time #blessed #grateful #nailingit."

The Social Media Show-Off has one mission: to curate a life that looks better than yours. Not actually *be* better—just *look* better. Their entire existence is a highlight reel. Behind the scenes? Chaos. On Instagram? Perfectly lit lattes, toned gym selfies, and captions stolen from Pinterest.

Family events are their content farms. They arrive with their phone fully charged, their ring light "just in case," and a look in their eyes that says, *You're all about to become props in my digital empire.* Before you can even take your coat off, they're demanding group photos, forcing you into awkward poses, and yelling, "No duck faces, guys—just be natural!" while they suck in their stomach and tilt their head to exactly the right angle.

And don't even think about eating before they've taken 97 pictures of the food. Turkey, pie, mashed potatoes—it's all cold by the time you get a bite because Captain Content needed the perfect shot. "Wait, don't touch the gravy yet—I need a boomerang!" By dessert, you're not just hungry, you're contemplating faking a medical emergency to escape the photo shoot.

The worst part? They narrate their own life like it's breaking news. "Just here with the fam, living our best lives!" they squeal into their phone, conveniently ignoring the fact that Aunt Linda is crying in the corner and Uncle Bob is asleep face-down on the couch. It's not about reality—it's about optics. If they can slap on a filter and throw in a hashtag, it's officially #amazing.

Every accomplishment is inflated. Got a new job? They'll announce it with a five-slide carousel, inspirational quotes, and at least three selfies in business attire. Ran a 5K? By the time they're done posting about it, you'd think they personally won the Boston Marathon. Even their kids aren't safe—they've been turned into tiny unpaid influencers, paraded online in matching outfits with captions like, "My mini-me, my everything #momlife #perfectchild." Meanwhile, the "perfect child" is screaming because someone took away their juice box.

And God forbid you achieve something before they do. If you post your vacation pictures, suddenly they're "spontaneously" booking a trip to Bali. If you announce a promotion, they're suddenly "transitioning into a leadership role." If you get engaged, they'll post a photo of themselves with the caption, "So happy for my bestie! Love wins!" followed by, "Also, can't wait to share MY big news soon..." Spoiler: there is no news. They're just allergic to not being the center of attention.

The Social Media Show-Off doesn't just want to live—they want to trend. They want to be envied, admired, and—most importantly—*liked*. Because in their world, likes are currency, followers are validation, and if it's not posted online, it didn't happen.

Buckle up, because if the in-laws made you feel judged and the Drunk Uncle made you feel violated, the Social Media Show-Off will make you feel like an unpaid extra in a reality show you never auditioned for.

Classic Moves

The Group Photo Hostage Situation.

The second they walk in, you're not family anymore—your unpaid models. They line you up, demand multiple angles, and scream "One more!" like they're Annie Leibovitz. Meanwhile, you're sweating under the dining room lights, blinking like a hostage in a ransom video, and praying the flash blinds you permanently.

The Food Photography Crimes.

Nobody eats until they've snapped 97 shots of the turkey, five boomerangs of the gravy pour, and one slow-mo video of pie being sliced. By the time you finally get to eat, the mashed potatoes are colder than your mother-in-law's smile.

The Humblebrag Caption.

Every post is a brag disguised as modesty. "Just a casual family dinner I threw together #nofilter #chefstatus." Translation: *Please validate me, strangers of the internet.* If they cured cancer, the caption would still be: "So honored to have been asked to help out, no biggie #blessed."

The Copy-Paste Quotes.

Their captions always come straight from Pinterest or motivational accounts. You'll see photos of them holding wine with text like, "She believed she could, so she did." Meanwhile, she believed she could cook, and she burned the rolls.

The Competitive Posting.

Heaven forbid you share your own good news. If you post about a new job, suddenly they've got a new "business venture." If you share your vacation pics, they're "spontaneously" booking tickets to Europe. It's not about celebration—it's about keeping up, one heavily filtered selfie at a time.

The Unpaid Influencer Children.

Their kids didn't sign up for Instagram stardom, but here they are, in matching outfits, posing with pumpkins, or holding signs like "First Day of School!" Meanwhile, those kids are sticky, screaming, and seconds away from a sugar-fueled meltdown. But online? #PerfectLife.

The Fake Reality Show.

Every gathering turns into a performance. They film clinking glasses, force everyone to shout "cheers!" in unison, and then narrate the evening like a host on Bravo. "Just here with the fam, making memories #squadgoals." In reality, half the "squad" wants to crawl under the table.

The Awkward Tagging.

No one is safe. You'll wake up to find yourself tagged in a close-up where you look like a sleep-deprived goblin. And when you complain? "Oh, but you look so *real!*" Translation: *I needed extras to make myself look better.*

The Social Media Show-Off doesn't live life. They stage it. And everyone else is just a blurry supporting character in their endless quest for validation.

How to Survive the Social Media Show-Off

The Social Media Show-Off can't be stopped. They can't be reasoned with. They don't care if you're mid-bite, mid-sneeze, or mid-breakdown—the content must flow. But with the right tactics, you can at least make their obsession a little less painful.

1. Perfect the Photobomb

If they insist on turning every gathering into a photoshoot, embrace chaos. Cross your eyes, stick out your tongue, or make bunny ears in the background. If you're going to be unwillingly tagged online, at least make it worth it. Bonus points if your ridiculous face gets more likes than their carefully curated pose.

2. The Strategic Blink

They want flawless pictures. Give them the opposite. Every time they snap, close your eyes just enough to look like you're falling asleep. After the fifth ruined group shot, they'll think twice before demanding "just one more!"

3. Enforce the No-Phones Rule

Declare it a "no devices" dinner. Collect everyone's phones in a basket at the door. Sure, they'll pout, sigh, and act like you've stripped them of oxygen, but you'll finally get to eat a hot meal without being told to "hold the gravy like that again for the boomerang."

4. Fake Bad Angles

Lean in with your chin tucked, slouch dramatically, or hold your fork like a caveman. If they're going to tag you, you might as well make sure the picture is so unflattering that *they* don't want to post it. Weaponize ugliness.

5. Deploy the "Wow, So Real" Comment

When they post their latest "candid" selfie, leave a comment that ruins the illusion. "Love how this was taken after your 19th retake!" or "Remember when you screamed at us not to move while you set up the lighting? Iconic." The truth is the best filter.

6. Hide the Ring Light

No light, no content. If you can sneak away their portable glow machine and stash it in a closet, you've bought yourself at least twenty minutes of peace. Without perfect lighting, their urge to post drops by half.

7. Turn Their Hashtags Against Them

If they flood your feed with #LivingMyBestLife, start replying with #SomeoneTakeHerPhone. If it's #FamilyGoals, comment with "Yeah, if your goal is cold mashed potatoes." Sometimes sarcasm is the only language they understand.

8. Bribe Them With Content

Sometimes the easiest way out is to play along. Snap a quick photo of them looking good, hand them their dopamine hit, and boom—they leave you alone for ten blessed minutes. Think of it as paying a toll.

9. Stage Your Own Revenge Post

Flip the script. Take your own candid shots of *them*—the double chin, the food stuck in their teeth, the dramatic selfie prep—and post it with the caption, "Behind the scenes with our influencer-in-training #authentic #nofilter." They'll either learn humility or plot your murder. Either way, it's worth it.

10. Remember: It's All Fake Anyway

The real secret? Accept that none of it matters. Their posts aren't reality—they're smoke, mirrors, and a touch of Photoshop. Once you stop caring about how you look in their feed, the whole circus loses its power. They can stage all the selfies they want; you'll be the one enjoying hot food while it's still warm.

The Wrap-Up

The Social Media Show-Off is less a family member and more a one-person marketing agency, churning out content no one asked for. They don't attend gatherings—they produce them. And while the rest of us are just trying to survive the day without indigestion, they're out here auditioning for the highlight reel of their own imaginary reality show.

What makes them so unbearable isn't just the endless selfies, the hashtags, or the group photo hostage situations. It's that they rob the moment of... well, the *moment*. Instead of laughing at Uncle Bob passing out in the recliner, you're forced to recreate it with better lighting. Instead of eating hot turkey, you're waiting while someone hovers over the table with a phone, whispering "Wait, wait, I just need one more angle." By the time you finally eat, the gravy's congealed into something that could be used as tile grout.

I once sat through a Christmas dinner where we didn't eat for thirty minutes because my cousin insisted on arranging the food "just so" for a perfect overhead shot. The cranberry sauce was shifted three times, the mashed potatoes were sculpted into a mountain, and the turkey was spun around like a runway model until it had "the right side facing the light." By the time she finally shouted, "Okay, got it!" half the family was on the verge of gnawing the table legs. The photo, of course, was captioned: *"Nothing better than a warm, cozy meal with the people I love most. #Grateful #Blessed."* The irony? Nobody looked cozy, nobody felt grateful, and the turkey was stone cold.

That's the Social Media Show-Off in a nutshell: it's never about reality, it's about optics. And while you might hate being dragged into their never-ending content machine, at least you'll have a story to tell—the one that doesn't make it onto Instagram.

So the next time they demand a group selfie, don't roll your eyes. Smile. Because years from now, when you're scrolling back through the chaos, those photos will remind you of the truth: family gatherings are messy, awkward, and full of weirdos. And no filter in the world can hide that.

CHAPTER ELEVEN
THE CONSPIRACY COUSIN

Welcome to the Rabbit Hole

Every dysfunctional circle has one. They might be related to you by blood, marriage, or sheer bad luck. They arrive at family gatherings, barbecues, and group chats armed with binders, links, and a suspicious amount of printer ink. They lower their voices as if the turkey itself is bugged, and they open conversations with phrases like *"I'm just saying..."* or *"If you knew what I know..."*

This is your **Conspiracy Cousin.**

The Conspiracy Cousin doesn't simply *question things*. No, that would make them reasonable. They don't just read Wikipedia at 3 a.m. and call it a night. Instead, they plunge headfirst into the rabbit hole and redecorate it with string maps, Reddit printouts, and a collection of YouTube playlists that somehow count as "peer-reviewed research."

Their defining trait? Confidence. Absolute, unshakeable confidence that they know The Truth™. Never mind that they failed high school physics, couldn't assemble IKEA furniture if their life depended on it, and once got scammed by a fake Netflix login page. Now, somehow, they're a leading expert on astrophysics, geopolitics, and "shadow organizations that control the price of corn."

You'll recognize them instantly. They always hover near the snack table (fuel is necessary for truth-seekers). Their eyes dart suspiciously whenever someone mentions the government, 5G, or gluten. And if you make the mistake of asking how they've been, congratulations: you've accidentally triggered a two-hour TED Talk titled *"Everything You Thought You Knew About Reality Is a Lie."*

Every encounter with them feels like you've wandered into a late-night cable documentary narrated by a man with a beard down to his ankles. Except now it's live, and you're the hostage audience.

But here's the kicker: The Conspiracy Cousin isn't just annoying. They're relentless. You can't escape them, because family dinners, weddings, office happy hours, and even funerals are fair game. Your great-aunt may be weeping at the casket, but Conspiracy Cousin is whispering, *"Did you know this whole thing is a cover-up?"*

It's exhausting. It's absurd. And it's also, if you squint hard enough, kind of hilarious.

This chapter is your guide to recognizing, managing, and ultimately surviving The Conspiracy Cousin. Think of it less as an intervention and more as an anthropological field manual. By the end, you'll know their classic moves, their greatest hits, and the survival tactics you'll need if you ever want to finish a holiday meal without being accused of being a government plant.

The Greatest Hits of Conspiracy Cousin

Like every recurring character in the soap opera of your social life, the Conspiracy Cousin has a *setlist.* These are the greatest hits, performed on loop, no matter the occasion. You've heard them before. You'll hear them again. And again. And again, until you start wishing you *had* been abducted by aliens just for the peace and quiet.

1. *The Moon Landing Was Faked*

The OG of conspiracies. According to your cousin, Neil Armstrong never set foot on the moon. It was all a Hollywood production, probably directed by Stanley Kubrick between takes of *The Shining.* "Look at the shadows," they'll whisper, pulling out a grainy photocopy. "Shadows don't lie." (Neither, apparently, does YouTube user TruthSeeker420.)

2. *Big Pharma Doesn't Want You to Know About...*

Turmeric. Pickle juice. Essential oils. Magic mushrooms. The "miracle cure" rotates weekly, but the theme is constant: if it glows, tingles, or costs $99.99 plus shipping, it will heal you instantly. The only reason you don't know this? Corporate greed, obviously. Never mind that Cousin Kyle once got food poisoning from gas-station sushi—he's practically a licensed naturopath now.

3. *Birds Aren't Real*

Yes, birds. According to Conspiracy Cousin, the entire pigeon population was replaced by government drones in the 1970s. "Think about it," they hiss. "When's the last time you saw a baby pigeon?" You resist the urge to answer, "When's the last time you touched grass?"

4. *The Earth Is Flat*

They failed geometry, but sure, they're now experts in astrophysics. Conspiracy Cousin will gleefully explain that NASA is lying, photos of Earth are fake, and airline pilots are "in on it." Meanwhile, you're trying not to choke on your stuffing.

5. *The Weather Machine*

Every time it rains on their birthday barbecue, it's not bad luck—it's the government testing HAARP. Thunderstorms? Engineered. Hurricanes? Designed for population control. Mild drizzle? Bill Gates, probably.

6. *The Secret Cabal*

This is the "choose your own adventure" of conspiracies. Sometimes it's lizard people. Sometimes it's billionaires. Sometimes it's the PTA. The only thing you can count on is that they're all working together, and your cousin is the lone whistleblower standing in their way.

Pro Tip: Conspiracy Cousins never stop at one theory. They collect them like Pokémon cards. The deeper they go, the more crossover episodes you get. Suddenly, the moon landing connects to Bigfoot, which links to gluten intolerance, which ties back to your uncle's hip replacement. It's the *Marvel Cinematic Universe* of paranoia—and you're trapped in the audience.

Classic Moves

The Holiday Hijack.
Every big meal is their stage. Christmas dinner? Perfect time to explain how Santa is a corporate psy-op invented by Coca-Cola. Thanksgiving? Actually a cover-up for crop experimentation. Easter? Don't even ask—you'll never look at chocolate bunnies the same way again.

The "I Did My Research" Speech.
Their favorite line. You might think "research" means peer-reviewed studies or credible sources. Not to them. To the Conspiracy Cousin, "research" means watching 12 hours of grainy YouTube videos narrated by someone named "TruthSeeker_420" and scrolling through Facebook groups with names like *The Real Truth They Don't Want You to Know.*

The Bird Truthers.
You thought pigeons were just annoying? Not to the Conspiracy Cousin. They'll whisper about government spy drones disguised as birds. They'll point at a seagull and mutter, "Look at its dead eyes. That's not natural." Family picnics quickly turn into suspicious glances at every sparrow within a ten-mile radius.

The Tap Water Tirade.
Every gathering includes a lecture about what's *really* in the water. "Fluoride isn't for your teeth—it's for your mind control." Suddenly, your cousin is sipping only bottled water they hauled in from a "safe source," which usually means a gas station two towns

over. Bonus points if they wear a necklace filled with "purifying crystals."

The Coded Message Hunt.

TV commercials, cereal boxes, movie posters—nothing is safe. To the Conspiracy Cousin, everything is a secret code. "See that logo? Triangle. Illuminati confirmed." Family game night with Scrabble devolves into them rearranging tiles into "hidden warnings."

The 5G Meltdown.

If the Wi-Fi is slow, brace yourself. They'll launch into a tirade about electromagnetic waves frying our brains. If someone so much as mentions upgrading their phone, you'll get a detailed rant about "radiation death beams." And of course, they'll proudly wave their "protective" phone case that looks suspiciously like a piece of tin foil wrapped in duct tape.

The Sheeple Shout.

Their favorite insult. If you disagree, you're a sheep. If you laugh, you're brainwashed. If you try to change the subject, you're "afraid of the truth." Basically, unless you join their crusade, you're livestock. The irony? They're the ones following every half-baked internet prophet they can find.

The Awkward Exit.

Eventually, someone snaps: "Can we please just eat in peace?" The Conspiracy Cousin will huff, declare the family "closed-minded," and storm off. Ten minutes later, they're back in the living room, casually eating pie—still muttering about chemtrails.

The Conspiracy Cousin doesn't just believe in alternative facts—they're powered by them. Every family gathering is another chance to spread the gospel of paranoia, one baffled relative at a time.

How to Survive the Conspiracy Cousin

No intervention. No argument. No amount of actual science is going to pry the tin-foil crown off your cousin's head. What you *can* do is learn survival tactics. Think of this section as your **Dysfunctional Lifehacks™**, tailored for maximum sanity preservation.

1. The Neutral Nod

Master this face: eyebrows slightly raised, lips pressed, chin tilted like you're hearing something profound. Add a quiet "Hmm." This says, *"I acknowledge your madness without signing the lease."* It buys you time until someone interrupts to ask who brought the pie.

2. Distract & Redirect

Conspiracy Cousin: "You know they're putting mind-control nanobots in toothpaste..."

You: "Wow, speaking of mint, did you try Aunt Karen's mojitos?"

This technique shifts the topic from "government fluoride experiments" to "cocktail hour" in three seconds flat.

3. The Preemptive Strike

Arrive locked and loaded with your own absurd theory. Example: "Did you hear IKEA is secretly training squirrels to replace delivery drivers?" One of two things will happen:

a) They'll laugh and shut up.

b) They'll nod seriously and recruit you.

Either way, you're no longer the hunted. You're playing offense.

4. The Humor Deflection

When all else fails, laugh. Loud, unbothered, belly deep. Treat their story about lizard overlords like it's peak stand-up. This either embarrasses them into silence... or fuels them. (Warning: only attempt if you're fast enough to dodge flying printouts.)

5. The Escape Route

Never enter a family gathering without knowing your exits. Bathrooms, patios, fake phone calls, *"Oh, I think my casserole is burning."* In extreme cases, train your phone to ring when you press the side button three times. Conspiracy Cousin can't fact-check Apple shortcuts.

6. The "Yes, And" Trap

Borrow from improv comedy. Instead of fighting, join in—but escalate to the point of absurdity.

Cousin: "The government controls the weather."

You: "Exactly, that's why I only barbecue on Tuesdays. They can't program Tuesdays."

The absurdity might short-circuit them. Or you'll end up as the co-founder of their next Facebook group. Roll the dice.

7. Divide and Conquer

Keep them busy. Strategically pair them with another relative who loves to argue. Release them into the wild like two feral cats. Then slip away quietly and enjoy dessert in peace.

8. The Acceptance Zen

At some point, you realize Conspiracy Cousin is never going to change. They've built their whole identity around these theories. Instead of resisting, lean back, sip your wine, and think of it as free performance art. You didn't buy tickets, but you're definitely at a show.

Remember: Your goal isn't to convert them to reality. Your goal is survival. Protect your sanity, secure your snacks, and make sure you leave the gathering with at least one-story worth retelling later.

Conspiracy Cousin in the Digital Age

Once upon a time, your exposure to Conspiracy Cousin was seasonal. A holiday here, a barbecue there. Now, thanks to smartphones, you're living in the golden age of unsolicited conspiracy content. They don't just ruin dinner—they ruin *Tuesday mornings, Sunday naps,* and every moment your phone buzzes at 2 a.m.

Your inbox, group chat, and Facebook feed are their stage. Prepare yourself for:

The Chain Bomb:
"Forward this to five people before they delete it!" Attached: a blurry PDF written by "Anonymous Patriot."

The Video Barrage:
Links to YouTube videos with titles like *"THE TRUTH ABOUT WATER (they don't want you to know!!!)"*. Each one is 47 minutes long, and each one begins with ominous music and ends with, "Wake up, sheeple."

The Comment Crusade:
They don't just share—they argue. Every Facebook post, no matter how innocent ("Happy birthday, Grandma!"), becomes a battleground. Soon you're watching them fight with strangers about lizard people in the comments of a cheesecake recipe.

The Meme Storm:
Conspiracy Cousin has mastered Canva. Expect pixelated memes with glowing eyes, flaming text, and eagles superimposed on pyra-

mids. None of them make sense. All of them are captioned *"Do your research."*

Digital Conspiracy Cousins are harder to escape. You can mute chats, unfollow them, or fake a phone upgrade, but they will find you. They'll create new accounts, join Telegram, or switch platforms entirely. Like mold, they adapt.

Pro Tip: If you must respond, reply with something harmless like *"Wow, that's wild."* Never, under any circumstances, type the word *"interesting."* To Conspiracy Cousin, that's blood in the water.

Case Studies in Chaos

Case Study #1: Patient Zero — Kyle at Thanksgiving

It was a peaceful scene. Turkey carved, cranberry sauce congealing, relatives lulled into a food coma. Then Kyle—our family's Conspiracy Cousin—cleared his throat.

"Did you know," he began, "that the government uses pumpkin pie spice to suppress free thought?"

No one made eye contact. Aunt Linda pretended to fuss with the gravy boat. Uncle Bob muttered something about football. But Kyle was just warming up. Within minutes, the table had been treated to a TED Talk about 5G, lizard people, and a PowerPoint presentation stored on his phone.

Survival outcome: three relatives fled to the patio, two faked urgent phone calls, and one elderly grandmother loudly announced she needed to use the restroom... for forty-five minutes.

Case Study #2: The Group Chat Meltdown of 2021

The family group chat had been peaceful for months—mostly baby photos, casserole recipes, and the occasional "Happy Birthday" gif. Then Cousin Dana dropped a link: *Top 10 Secrets the CDC Won't Tell You.*"

Within hours, the chat had devolved into a battlefield. Emojis were weaponized. Caps lock became the language of war. At one point, Aunt Cheryl posted nothing but 17 angry face emojis in a row.

The group chat split into factions: Team Science, Team "Do Your Own Research," and Team "Please Stop, I Just Wanted the Cookie Recipe." The chat was eventually renamed "Potluck Planning" in an attempt to reset. Dana simply created a spin-off chat called "Truth Seekers Only."

Survival outcome: most of the family quietly muted both chats and now communicate exclusively through Venmo comments.

Case Study #3: The Wedding Reception Incident

During the father-daughter dance, Cousin Matt seized the microphone from the DJ. Instead of toasts or warm wishes, guests received a 12-minute lecture on how wedding rings are actually "tracking devices installed by the diamond cartel."

The bride cried. The groom drank. The DJ unplugged the mic halfway through. Matt swore this was proof they were silencing him.

Survival outcome: the couple eloped to Vegas two months later.

Lesson: Wherever people gather, Conspiracy Cousin lurks. You can't stop them. You can only document their behavior, adapt, and pray for Wi-Fi outages.

Conspiracy Cousin Bingo

Survival is easier when you turn it into a game. Next time you're trapped at a gathering, slip this card under the table and play along.

BINGO Squares:

Mentions "sheeple."

Uses the phrase "Do your own research."

Brings a laminated chart.

Says "NASA lies."

Whispers like the gravy boat is bugged.

Wears a slogan hat ("Don't Trust Birds").

Drops "Big Pharma" at least once.

Claims the weather is engineered.

Shows you a video longer than 30 minutes.

Tells you you've been "programmed."

Bonus: Shout "BINGO!" when you win. They'll assume you've cracked the code, not the game.

The Wrap-Up

The Conspiracy Cousin isn't really a relative so much as a walking podcast episode no one subscribed to. They don't attend gatherings to connect—they attend to enlighten (read: lecture) the "sheeple." And while the rest of us are just trying to survive without indigestion, they're out here auditioning for the role of "Main Character in Humanity's Final Battle."

What makes them so unbearable isn't just the endless theories, the whispered warnings, or the unsolicited video screenings. It's that they hijack the moment. Instead of laughing at Uncle Bob passing out in the recliner, you're forced to endure a tangent about how recliners were invented to weaken the human spine. Instead of eating hot turkey, you're waiting while someone explains how Thanksgiving is secretly sponsored by Big Corn. By the time they finally run out of breath, the gravy's congealed into something NASA could use to seal a rocket.

I once sat through a birthday dinner where we didn't cut the cake for forty minutes because my cousin was proving the frosting pattern was a "coded message from the Illuminati." The poor cake was rotated, examined, and photographed from every angle like it was evidence in a crime scene. By the time we finally ate it, the candles had melted into wax puddles and half the guests were debating whether to chew the table decorations. The kicker? He left the party early to "upload his findings."

That's Conspiracy Cousin in a nutshell: it's never about reality, it's about revelation. And while you might hate being dragged into their truth-seeking circus, at least you'll have a story to tell—the one that doesn't end with "Wake up, sheeple."

So the next time they lean in with wide eyes and whisper, "You know this is all a cover-up, right?" don't argue. Just smile. Because years from now, when you're retelling the madness, those moments will remind you of the truth: gatherings are messy, awkward, and full of weirdos. And no amount of "research" can hide that.

CHAPTER TWELVE

MEET THE
PET PARENT
EXTREMIST

Every dysfunctional circle has one: the person who believes their dog is not just a pet but a reincarnated monarch, a guru, or at minimum, the most important member of the family. This is **The Pet Parent Extremist.**

They don't simply *own* pets — they curate them. These creatures are styled, accessorized, photographed, and narrated with the gravity usually reserved for actual human children. The Pet Parent Extremist refers to their Shih Tzu as "my daughter," their iguana as "my little prince," and their cat as "my spiritual advisor." If you dare say "dog," they will correct you with a wounded gasp: *"Excuse me, she's my baby."*

You'll spot them instantly at gatherings. Not because of their outfits, but because of the entourage. They never arrive solo. They arrive with Muffin in a stroller, Coco in a sling, or Baxter the Bearded Dragon in a seasonal sweater. The air is filled with jingling tags, squeaky toys, and the faint smell of organic salmon treats.

And make no mistake — you are expected to play along. Forget greeting the human. You must crouch down, coo in baby talk, and acknowledge that Muffin *"has such a big personality."* Failure to do so is social suicide. The Pet Parent Extremist will glare as though you just insulted their firstborn child. Which, in their mind, you did.

What makes them so exhausting isn't their love of animals — animals are great. It's their *insistence* that everyone else loves them *equally*, on demand, and with the same deranged devotion. You can't just say, "Cute dog." No, you must have a full conversation about Muffin's "opinions on the current political climate" and validate that she really *does* look slimmer since switching to raw food.

The Pet Parent Extremist is not content with a quick pat on the head. They want a standing ovation for Muffin's new haircut. They want you to watch videos of Bella's agility training. They want you to sign a card for their cat's birthday. They want you to clap when Daisy eats kale.

This chapter is your manual for surviving them. You'll learn their classic moves, their greatest hits, and the coping strategies that will keep you sane while your wine mysteriously fills with cat hair. Think of it as your safari guide to the domestic jungle — because once the Pet Parent Extremist arrives, every event turns into a pet parade you never bought tickets for.

Classic Moves

Like every repeat offender in the dysfunctional circus, The Pet Parent Extremist comes with a predictable repertoire. These are the behaviors you'll see at every gathering — watch carefully, and you'll spot them before you find yourself cooing at a dog in a bow tie.

1. The Fur Baby Correction

You made the rookie mistake of calling Muffin "a dog."

Wrong.

The Pet Parent Extremist will gasp like you insulted a royal bloodline. "Excuse me," they'll say, "she's my *daughter*." Suddenly, you're expected to apologize to a Chihuahua wearing rhinestones.

2. The Event Plus-One (or Plus-Four)

Weddings, funerals, baptisms — no event is off-limits. Where you see a formal occasion, they see an opportunity to showcase Coco's new tuxedo. Your cousin's engagement party? Now featuring a pug in a bow tie. Grandma's funeral? Don't worry, the cat's in mourning too — she's wearing black.

3. The Menu Modification

Dinner isn't about you anymore. It's about Muffin's dairy sensitivity. Potatoes must be remade with oat milk. Desserts must be pet-safe. Someone will try to sneak kibble into the charcuterie board. If you forget, you'll be reminded that "Bella has allergies."

4. The Vet Flex

The rest of us talk about doctors. They talk about veterinarians. "Dr. Thompson says Muffin is *very advanced for her age.*" "Dr. Patel thinks Luna might be gifted." Their vet isn't a service provider — they're basically a co-parent.

5. The Holiday Hijacker

What's Christmas without a stocking for every pet? What's Easter without dog-friendly chocolate substitutes? Thanksgiving dinner halts while everyone claps as Daisy the Golden Retriever "says grace" with a paw trick.

6. The Photo Shoot Takeover

You thought you were taking a simple group photo. Nope. Now you're waiting while Muffin is adjusted for lighting, Baxter's sweater is straightened, and Coco the pug is positioned "on her good side." Thirty minutes later, you're smiling through clenched teeth while holding a ferret in a bow tie.

Survival Strategies

You can't cure them. You can't stop them. You can only *manage your exposure.* Here are the essential strategies for surviving The Pet Parent Extremist without losing your sanity (or your drink to a curious snout).

1. Greet the Royalty First

Forget handshakes, hugs, or polite small talk. Your first words must be directed at Muffin, Princess, or Baxter. Say hello. Scratch ears. Compliment the outfit. Only then are you permitted to acknowledge the human attached to the leash.

2. Compliment the Accessories

Your opinion on Muffin's sequined harness matters more than your opinion on politics, religion, or the economy. The safest line? *"Wow, that collar is stunning — where did you find it?"* (Answer: an Etsy shop that charges more than your rent.)

3. Prepare Universal Praise

The golden phrase is: *"She has such a big personality."* Use it often. It works whether the animal is staring blankly into space, gnawing on a shoe, or lunging at your plate.

4. BYO Lint Roller

You *will* leave covered in fur. Plan ahead. Slide a lint roller into your bag or car. Consider carrying two: one for before the event, one for after. (Pro tip: don't wear black. Ever.)

5. Deploy Strategic Distractions

When the Pet Parent Extremist launches into Muffin's "wellness journey," interrupt with something shiny. *"Oh wow, did someone just open the wine?"* or *"Hey, wasn't there a rumor about karaoke later?"* This works best if paired with a quick escape to the bathroom.

6. Create a Safe Zone

Find the other relatives equally exhausted by the pet circus. Band together in the garage, the patio, or anywhere Muffin's stroller can't fit. Share snacks. Whisper support. It's basically a survivor's bunker.

7. Fake Allergies (Extreme Tactic)

When all else fails, claim you're "allergic." Warning: this may trigger lectures about "holistic cures" or "hypoallergenic breeds." Proceed with caution — but sometimes a sneeze buys you freedom.

8. Reframe the Chaos

Instead of seething, treat it as free comedy. You didn't sign up for dinner theater, but you're in the audience now. Take mental notes. Collect lines. You'll be the hit of your next party when you tell the story of the Shih Tzu who got a birthday cake bigger than your niece's.

Remember: you're not here to fix them. You're here to preserve your sanity and your food. And if that means clapping while a cat in a bonnet gets wheeled through the living room, so be it. Survival requires sacrifice.

Real Events by These Crazies

#1: The Wedding Paw-posal
Location: backyard engagement party.
Event Status: hijacked.
As the bride-to-be waited for her big moment, a bulldog named Bruno waddled in with a velvet ring box strapped to his back. The crowd "aww'd," the groom smiled nervously, and the bride whispered later that she was 70% sure Bruno was going to eat the ring. The Pet Parent Extremist swore this made the proposal "historic." The couple quietly admitted they would have preferred champagne.

#2: The Bark-Mitzvah
Yes, it happened. Complete with yarmulkes, organic bone-shaped cookies, and a rabbi who looked like he wanted to disappear into the carpet. Guests sang Hebrew prayers while Bella the labradoodle wore a custom satin cape. The human children at the event ate plain crackers and stared into the void.

#3: The Cat as Ring Bearer

At a garden wedding, the Pet Parent Extremist insisted Princess the Siamese be the ring bearer. The cat was carried down the aisle in a velvet-lined basket, hissing like she'd been possessed by demons. When the rings were finally retrieved, the minister had claw marks. The photos were captioned *"A perfect day. #MeowAndForever."*

#4: The Puppy Shower

Forget baby showers. This was for a golden retriever puppy named Bentley. There were gifts (monogrammed sweaters), party games ("Pin the Tail on the Human"), and a cake made of beef liver. Guests smiled politely while quietly Googling: *"How long do I have to stay at a dog shower before it's socially acceptable to leave?"*

#5: The Thanksgiving Incident

Dinner was delayed 45 minutes because Muffin the Shih Tzu had to "say grace." This involved the Pet Parent Extremist holding Muffin's paw over the turkey and whispering a blessing. By the time forks hit plates, the gravy had cooled to the consistency of tile grout.

Conclusion: The Pet Parent Extremist doesn't attend events — they stage productions starring animals. Your job is not to stop them. Your job is to collect stories. Because one day, you'll be at a bar telling the tale of the Bark-Mitzvah, and everyone will beg you to write it down.

The Wrap-Up

The Pet Parent Extremist isn't so much a family member as a full-blown animal PR agency. They don't attend gatherings — they curate events where their pets are the headliners and the rest of us are just background extras. And while you're trying to make

it through the night without fur in your wine, they're busy orches-
trating Muffin's grand entrance in a rhinestone collar.

What makes them unbearable isn't the animals (everyone likes
pets). It's the insistence that you treat them as equals — or worse,
superiors. Suddenly, you're clapping for a dog eating kale, holding
a cat in a stroller, and nodding gravely as someone explains their
parrot is "still grieving." By the time dessert arrives, you're questioning your life choices.

I once sat through a Thanksgiving where we delayed dinner
because Muffin had to "bless the meal." A paw was placed solemnly
over the turkey, everyone bowed their heads, and the gravy congealed into something that could patch drywall. Later, the Pet
Parent Extremist posted on Instagram: *"Nothing more meaningful
than family gathered together. #FurEverFamily #Blessed."* Meanwhile, half the room was Googling "nearest Chinese takeout open
on holidays."

That's The Pet Parent Extremist in a nutshell: it's never about
reality, it's about optics. And while you may hate being drafted
into their never-ending pet-centric theater, at least you'll have a
story to tell — the unfiltered version that doesn't make it onto
Instagram.

So next time they demand a group selfie with a pug in a bow
tie, don't roll your eyes. Smile. Because years from now, when
you're retelling the chaos, you'll remember the truth: gatherings
are messy, awkward, and full of weirdos — even the four-legged
ones. And no filter in the world can hide that.

Chapter Thirteen

Conclusion: A Final Toast to Dysfunction

The Closing Ceremony

Every great circus needs a finale, and every Olympics needs a closing ceremony. So here we are, standing in the confetti of roast chicken bones, casserole crumbs, and broken wine glasses, ready to hand out medals for excellence in dysfunction.

The Drama Queen wins gold in *Theatrical Overreaction,* clutching her bouquet of imaginary roses while sighing dramatically about how nobody clapped loudly enough.

The Moocher takes silver in *Unpaid Consumption,* balancing six Tupperware containers like trophies and still asking, "Is there more?"

The Drunk Uncle stumbles in for bronze, half-asleep and still holding a beer, insisting he was "robbed by the judges."

The Guilt Tripper gets a Lifetime Achievement Award for *Emotional Manipulation,* because honestly, they've been training since birth.

The Toxic Friend doesn't get a medal—they just steal yours, then complain it doesn't fit right.

The In-Law Olympics earn a group ribbon for *Most Relentless Judging,* since they never agree on anything long enough to accept individual awards.

The Social Media Show-Off gets a special plaque for *Content Farming Under Hostage Conditions,* though they'll crop the rest of us out of the photo.

The Conspiracy Cousin demanded an award but refused to accept it, claiming the medals are microchipped.

The Pet Parent Extremist receives a custom collar and matching tiara—for their dog.

And finally, **you**—the reader—get the real gold medal. Because while the rest of your family/friends/in-laws are out here perfecting their dysfunction, you had the guts (and sense of humor) to face it head-on. You survived the pageant of weirdness, the buffet of bad behavior, the marathon of madness. And you did it without flipping a table. (Hopefully.)

Why We Laugh (Instead of Cry)

Here's the truth nobody puts in Hallmark cards: family, friends, and in-laws will drive you absolutely insane. They'll test your patience, poke your insecurities, and derail your holidays like professional demolition crews. If you take it too seriously, you'll end up rocking in the corner, muttering, "Why me?" while someone in the kitchen critiques your gravy.

That's why we laugh.

We don't laugh because the dysfunction disappears—it doesn't. Aunt Linda is still going to ask invasive questions about your love life. The Drunk Uncle is still going to try karaoke after his seventh beer. The Guilt Tripper will always sigh just loudly enough to make you feel like garbage. The chaos is permanent. What changes is how we *frame it.*

Humor is the buffer. It's the shield that takes the sting out of passive-aggression and turns it into material. Every cutting remark, every awkward silence, every meltdown—it all becomes part of the highlight reel. Instead of carrying the weight, you spin it into a story. Instead of feeling crushed, you lean into the absurdity.

Think about it: the disasters are the stories you actually tell later. Nobody reminisces about the smooth, drama-free Thanksgiving where the turkey was perfect and everyone agreed on politics. That memory disappears faster than a plate of deviled eggs. But the year your cousin stormed out screaming about chemtrails? Legendary. The time your dad tried to deep-fry a turkey and nearly set the garage on fire? Family lore.

Laughter doesn't erase the dysfunction—it transforms it. It gives you control, even when the situation is a circus. Once you can laugh, you're no longer the victim of the drama—you're the commentator, calling the play-by-play with a smirk and a glass of wine.

So why do we laugh instead of cry? Because crying gives you puffy eyes, but laughter gives you survival. And honestly, in a world where even your pets are showing up in bow ties for family dinner, survival is the real prize.

The Secret Upside of Dysfunction

Here's the plot twist nobody sees coming: dysfunction isn't just unavoidable—it's useful. As much as we groan, sigh, and plot fake emergencies to escape family dinners, the truth is that the weirdos are what make it memorable.

Think about it. A family gathering without the Drama Queen? Quiet, but flat. Without the Drunk Uncle? Safe, but boring. Without the Moocher? You'd have leftovers, sure—but no story to tell. Dysfunction is seasoning. Too much and it'll overwhelm the dish, but the right sprinkle keeps life spicy.

The chaos is where the stories live. Years from now, you won't remember what side dish you made in 2023. But you'll remember the night your Conspiracy Cousin tried to convince everyone the cranberry sauce was engineered by Big Pharma. You won't remember the exact outfit you wore to your cousin's wedding, but you'll never forget when the Social Media Show-Off turned the dance floor into a TikTok set. Dysfunction turns ordinary events into legendary tales.

And let's be honest—it's also the glue. Nothing bonds a group of otherwise rational people like collectively surviving the nonsense. You roll your eyes together, you exchange side glances, you share whispered sarcasm under the table. Dysfunction creates unity in the strangest way. You might not agree on politics, parenting, or pineapple on pizza—but you all agree that Uncle Bob should never be allowed near karaoke again.

Here's the real upside: dysfunction gives us perspective. It teaches us patience, sharpens our sense of humor, and makes us experts in emotional dodgeball. It forces us to see people as they really are—messy, flawed, human. And sometimes, that's comforting. Because if your family's a circus, you're not alone. We're all under the same dysfunctional big top.

So yes, dysfunction is maddening. But it's also bonding. It's storytelling fuel. It's the spice rack of life—chaotic, unbalanced, occasionally expired, but impossible to live without.

The Dysfunctional Survival Oath

Please rise, place your hand on the nearest casserole dish, and repeat after me:

I solemnly swear to survive my family, friends, and in-laws with sarcasm, snacks, and strategic bathroom breaks.

I pledge to recognize the Drama Queen's tears as theater, the Drunk Uncle's jokes as health hazards, and the Guilt Tripper's sighs as background noise.

I promise to never loan the Moocher anything I actually want back, to nod politely at the Conspiracy Cousin until dessert is served, and to comment "That's interesting" whenever an in-law critiques my life choices.

I vow to photobomb the Social Media Show-Off, to smile through the In-Law Olympics, and to applaud the Pet Parent Extremist's fur baby as if it really is a genius.

I commit to laughing instead of crying, roasting instead of raging, and drinking instead of debating (responsibly, of course).

And finally—

I accept that dysfunction is forever. I cannot escape it, out-argue it, or fix it. But I *can* collect it, roast it, and retell it until it becomes comedy gold.

By the power vested in sarcasm, snacks, and survival instincts:

Congratulations. You are now a Certified Dysfunctional Survivor.

The Final Toast

And so, we raise our glasses—not because we've solved anything (we haven't), not because anyone has changed (they won't), but because we've made it through the circus with our humor intact.

To the **Drama Queens**—may their tears never smudge waterproof mascara.

To the **Moochers**—may their hands forever be empty, and your fridge forever be locked.

To the **Drunk Uncles**—may their stories remain exaggerated, their pants zipped, and their karaoke machines unplugged.

To the **Guilt Trippers**—may their sighs bounce off your armor like Nerf darts.

To the **Toxic Friends**—may they ghost themselves before you have to.

To the **In-Laws**—may their scorecards catch fire in the candle centerpiece.

To the **Social Media Show-Offs**—may their ring lights burn out mid-selfie.

To the **Conspiracy Cousins**—may their tinfoil hats attract only good radio stations.

To the **Pet Parent Extremists**—may their fur babies live long, healthy lives—outside of the dinner table.

And to **you**—the reader who survived this dysfunctional parade: may you laugh louder, sigh less, and remember that you're not alone in the madness. We are all sitting at different tables in different houses, but somehow, it's the same circus.

Because in the end, dysfunction is universal. It's messy, maddening, absurd—and kind of beautiful in its own twisted way. These weirdos, these disasters, these self-proclaimed experts in chaos—they're ours. And without them, life would be unbearably bland.

So here's to the families, the friends, the in-laws, and the unwanted plus-ones. Here's to the arguments, the awkward silences, the karaoke disasters, and the turkey fires. Here's to the dysfunction that drives us crazy but also gives us the stories we'll laugh at forever.

Raise your glass high. Drink to survival. Drink to laughter. Drink to the circus we call life.

And as the curtain falls, remember: the weirdos are waiting. Always.

FAMILY & FRIENDS SURVIVAL GLOSSARY

Because sometimes words fail you, and other times you just need new ones to survive the circus. Use this as your translation guide to dysfunctional gatherings.

Backhanded Compliment Toss

The Olympic sport of saying something nice while actually stabbing you in the soul. Example: *"That haircut really... stands out."*

Bingo Moment

The exact second a relative fulfills their cliché role at a gathering. (See: Drama Queen Sigh, Moocher Raid, Drunk Uncle Toast.)

Burnt Offering

Any dish ruined by distraction, arguments, or alcohol. Usually still served with pride.

Coal Mine Bragger

A One-Upper who makes even your worst story sound like a spa day. You broke your arm? They broke both legs—while saving a bus of orphans.

Conspiracy Corner

The part of the living room where the Conspiracy Cousin sets up camp with their binder, laptop, and bad Wi-Fi takes.

Emotional Arsonist

A person who sets fire to peaceful situations just to watch the chaos burn. Commonly found in Drama Queens.

Faux Apology

"I'm sorry you feel that way." Translation: I'm not sorry, and I will absolutely do it again.

Fridge Raider

A Moocher who treats your kitchen like an all-you-can-eat buffet. Always leaves with leftovers, never returns Tupperware.

Gaslight Gala

A family debate where reality is casually rewritten. ("Nobody remembers it that way.")

Guilt Grenade

A sigh, a pause, or a loaded *"Don't worry about me..."* Weaponized guilt that explodes without warning.

Holiday Hunger Games

Annual holiday gathering where survival depends on dodging questions, hoarding rolls, and not flipping the table.

In-Law Olympics

The grueling competition where casseroles are critiqued, life choices are judged, and the scoring system is rigged.

Leftover Larceny

When someone "accidentally" leaves with the best food packed neatly in your containers.

Nap Bomb

When the Drunk Uncle passes out on the couch and snores so loudly it rattles the windows, but waking him is more dangerous than the noise.

One-Upper Overtime

The endless extension of conversations because one person always has a "better" story.

Passive-Aggressive Relay

The multi-generational sport of delivering insults disguised as kindness. Handed down like fine china.

Potluck Betrayal

When someone shows up with store-bought coleslaw in a crystal bowl and calls it "homemade."

Secondhand Spotlight

The Pet Parent Extremist's ability to shift focus away from humans and onto Muffin the Shih Tzu's new haircut.

Silent Stare Showdown

An unblinking glare from an in-law that communicates ten paragraphs of judgment without a single word.

Small Talk Smackdown

That moment when you've been cornered by someone determined to discuss weather, traffic, or lawn care for an hour.

Social Media Hijack

When the Social Media Show-Off turns a normal meal into a hostage photoshoot. Warning: food will be cold by the time you eat.

Subtle Sabotage

When your dish mysteriously gets moved to the "side table" or someone conveniently forgets to mention you brought dessert.

Tupperware Tax

The unspoken reality that any container lent to a Moocher is never coming back. Ever.

Unsolicited Life Coach

That relative who tells you what career, partner, and haircut you *should* have—unprompted.

Vacation Vultures

Family members who mysteriously become "best friends" when you mention you're renting a beach house.

Wine Shield

The only true defense against relatives. Deploy liberally, refill often.

Zoom Zombie

A cousin who spends the entire gathering scrolling TikTok, then claims later that "it was so nice catching up."

UNIVERSAL SURVIVAL TOOLKIT

Every dysfunctional gathering requires gear. You wouldn't hike Everest without supplies, so don't walk into Thanksgiving dinner without protection. Below is your essential checklist for surviving the people you can't escape. Print it. Laminate it. Hide it in your glove compartment for emergencies.

One Bottle of Cheap Wine (for Sharing)

Everyone gets a splash. It's the social lubricant that buys you 20 minutes of peace before the chaos begins.

One Bottle of Good Wine (for Hiding)

This is *yours*. Stash it in a travel mug, the garage, or behind the cranberry sauce. Do not share. Do not confess. This is your lifeline.

Emotional Earplugs

Not literal foam plugs (though those help). These are the invisible shields you deploy when someone starts a sentence with *"Back in my day..."* or *"So when are you having kids?"*

A Back-Pocket Excuse

"Oh no, I left something in the car."

"Oh no, I left something in the oven."

"Oh no, I left something in 2007."

Any of these will buy you at least five minutes of escape.

Snacks for Self-Soothing

Chocolate, chips, cookies—whatever works. These aren't for sharing; they're emergency rations. Hide them in your bag like contraband.

A Notebook for Bingo and Tallying One-Upper Points

Turn bragging into a sport. Assign points. Keep score. Award fake medals. Survival is easier when it feels like a game.

The Distraction Device

A phone loaded with memes, fake calls, and the Uber app. This is your digital parachute.

Lint Roller

For Pet Parent Extremist visits. You will leave covered in fur. Accept it, plan for it, and de-fur before public appearances.

Designated Safe Zone

Scout in advance: garage, patio, bathroom, or anywhere the Drunk Uncle can't find you. Claim it early, guard it fiercely.

The Sarcasm Shield

A handful of one-liners to deflect passive-aggressive attacks. Examples:

"Wow, that's fascinating."

"I'll take that under advisement."

"Thank you for your unsolicited TED Talk."

A Time-Limit Alarm

Set a hidden timer on your phone. When it goes off, you're allowed to leave—no guilt, no apologies. Survival has a schedule.

Final Note: You don't need every tool for every event. But you *do* need to know which combination will get you through unscathed. Choose wisely. Pack light. And never, ever forget the snacks.

Acknowledgements

First, thank you to my family and friends for being the endless circus that made this book possible. You provided the material, the meltdowns, and the mashed potato fights. Without you, I'd have nothing to roast (and way fewer therapy bills).

A special thanks to:

Wine — for being cheaper than therapy and more effective than patience.

Snacks — the true heroes of every survival strategy.

My Group Chat — for proving, daily, that chaos never takes a holiday.

Google — for teaching me whether you can survive four hours in close proximity to a Drama Queen without permanent damage.

All the Unsolicited Advice-Givers — thanks for reminding me what *not* to do. Ever.

And finally, thanks to you, dear reader, for picking up this guide. May it help you survive reunions, holidays, weddings, funerals, and that one cousin's MLM pitch disguised as a barbecue invite.

www.ingramcontent.com/pod-product-compliance
Lightning Source LLC
Chambersburg PA
CBHW070804290326
41931CB00011BA/2131